Handbook of Crochet Stitches

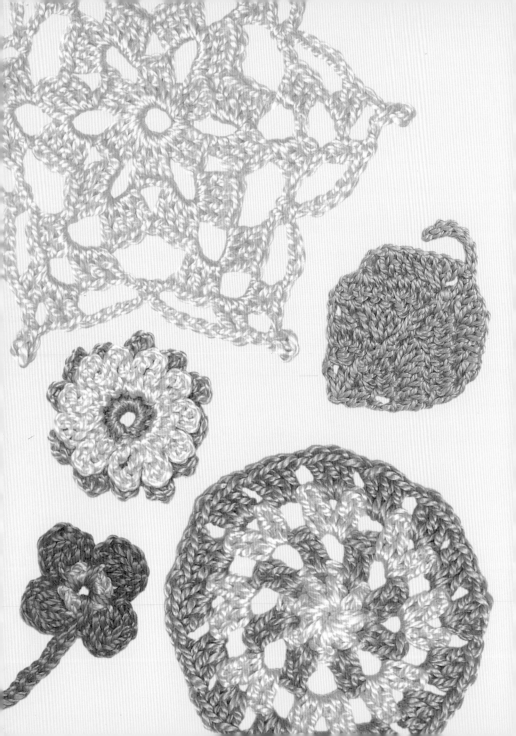

Handbook of Crochet Stitches

The complete illustrated reference to over 200 stitches

Betty Barnden

Search Press

A QUARTO BOOK

Published in 2009 by Search Press Ltd
Wellwood
North Farm Road
Tunbridge Wells
Kent TN2 3DR

Reprinted 2010

ISBN 978-1-84448-511-6

QUAR.CST

Conceived, designed and
produced by
Quarto Publishing plc
The Old Brewery
6 Blundell Street
London N7 9BH

Project Editors Fiona Robertson,
Liz Pasfield
Art Editor and Designer Julie Francis
Assistant Art Director Penny Cobb
Illustrators Kuo Kang Chen,
Coral Mula
Photographers Paul Forrester,
Colin Bowling
Pattern Checker Hazel Williams
Proofreader Gillian Haslam

Art Director Moira Clinch
Publisher Piers Spence

Manufactured by Modern Age
Repro House Ltd, Hong Kong

Printed in China by Midas Printing
International Ltd

Contents

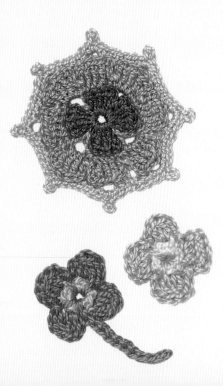

The Stitch Collection 52

Introduction

Crochet is the technique of making a looped fabric from a continuous length of yarn, using a single hook. The word "crochet" itself derives from the French "croc", meaning a hook (or crook); an old Scottish name for crochet is "shepherd's knitting". It is one of the most portable and flexible of crafts, requiring only a hook and some yarn; once you have mastered the basic techniques, you can create a fascinating variety of effects.

You only need a hook and some yarn to get started.

Like all the textile arts, the origins of crochet are obscure and only a few early examples remain; these have been found across the world, from China to Africa, Turkey, Europe, the United States and South America.

There is a wide variety of yarns available to choose from.

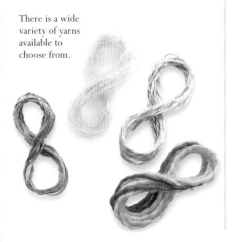

Most early examples are tightly worked with heavy yarns to create firm fabrics, often worked into fitted forms such as caps and hats. Wool yarns worked densely in this way were also used to make warm, windproof cloaks and blankets.

In sixteenth-century Italy, nuns developed the use of very fine steel hooks and cotton or linen yarns to create delicate, lace-like effects for trimmings and church vestments. This technique spread across Europe, notably to Ireland, and by the nineteenth century crochet lace was widely used for garments, trimmings

such as collars and cuffs, and household items such as tablecloths.

Over the centuries, many different stitch patterns and techniques have developed that we can use today in any way we please. Over 200 examples are included in this book, from basic firm fabrics to lacy squares and motifs. Use the Stitch Selector (page 44) to find a suitable stitch, then look up the detailed instructions in the Stitch Collection (page 52). In Crochet Essentials (page 10) you will find descriptions of the simple equipment and

Clockwise from far left: Chain loop stitch, Tunisian basketweave, Back raised trebles, Open ridge stitch, Broomstick lace, and Treble rounds.

materials needed for crochet. Choose from the wide variety of threads and yarns available today, or experiment with more unusual materials. You can make sweaters, hats, shawls, afghans, cushions, all with that special personal touch, unique to you.

Read this book with a hook and ball of yarn close at hand and be prepared to get hooked!

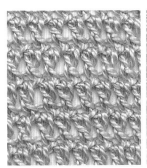

Introduction

How to use this book

Stitch patterns are organised into 14 sections. Detailed instructions and a stitch diagram accompany the photograph of each stitch sample.

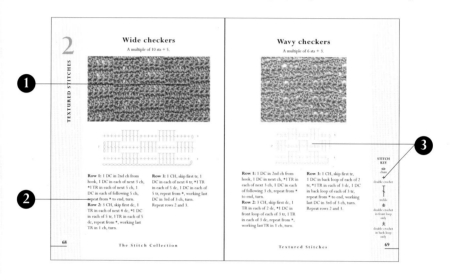

1 **Swatches**
Photographed and reproduced at 100 per cent (or where space does not permit this, as close to 100 per cent as possible) to provide an accurate impression of the finished design.

2 **Instructions**
Basic patterns are worked over any number of stitches, but repeating patterns require a multiple of a certain number as shown above the swatch photograph: e.g., "multiple of

3 sts + 2" means any number that divides by 3, with 2 more added, such as 9 + 2 (= 11) or 33 + 2 (= 35).

Extra stitches are sometimes required for the foundation chain: e.g., "multiple of 3 sts + 2 (add 2 for foundation ch)" means begin with a number of foundation chain that divides by 3, add 2, then add 2 more, such as 33 + 2 + 2 (= 37). Unless otherwise stated, all stitch patterns begin with a right side row.

Abbreviations

A full list is given on pages 248-249 In this book, abbreviations in capital letters (e.g., 1 DC) are the stitches you work on the current row, while abbreviations in lower case letters (e.g., dc) are previous stitches that are worked into or skipped: e.g., "1 DC in next tr" means "work one double crochet into the next treble of the row below".

Brackets and Asterisks

• *Square brackets* [ ] can mean:
1. Read as a group together: e.g., "skip [1 dc, 1 tr]" means skip 1 dc, skip 1 tr.
2. Repeat as given after the brackets: e.g., "[2 TR in next tr, 1 CH] twice" means 2 TR in next tr, 1 CH, 2 TR in following tr, 1 CH.
• *Curved brackets* ( ) are explanatory: e.g., 1 TR in next tr (the centre tr of 5) positions the stitch correctly.
• *Asterisks* * indicate the point from which instructions are repeated, either along a whole row, or just the number of times given:
e.g., "Repeat from * to end" means repeat the instructions after the *, to the end of the row; whereas "1 CH, * 1 DC in next ch, 1 TR in next ch, repeat from * once more" means "1 CH, 1 DC in next ch, 1 TR in next ch, 1 DC in next ch, 1 TR in next ch".

Where instructions given after the * do not fit exactly, or if a different stitch is worked at the end of the row, the instructions will read "repeat from *, ending (for example) 1 TR in last dc". E.g., "* 1 DC in next dc, 2 TR in next dc, repeat from * ending 1 TR in last dc" means repeat the instructions after the * but at the end of the last repeat, work only 1 TR in the last dc.

❸ Stitch Diagrams

A full list of stitch symbols is given on pages 248-250. A stitch diagram represents the right side of the work. Diagrams for patterns worked in rows show at least one complete pattern repeat, plus the stitches at each edge. Right side rows are numbered at the right and read from right to left. Wrong side rows are numbered at the left and read from left to right.

Rounds are numbered close to where they begin and read anti-clockwise, corresponding to the direction of work.

Always read the stitch diagram with the text.

Crochet Essentials

In this section you will find a guide to equipment and materials needed for crochet as well as descriptions of the basic stitches used.

Equipment and Materials

The hooks

Crochet hooks may be made from aluminium, steel, wood, bamboo, or plastic. They are available in a variety of sizes to suit different types of yarn and to enable you to make your stitches larger or smaller (see Measuring Tension, page 42). Sizes range from 0.6mm (the smallest) up to 15mm or more, and the hooks are normally between 5 in. (125mm) and 8 in. (200mm) long. The shaft behind the hook may be cylindrical, or with a flattened area to help you hold it at the correct angle. Try out the different options to decide which suits you best.

Crochet hooks are available in a wide range of sizes.

Hook sizes

The internationally used metric system of sizing known as the International Standard Range (ISR) gives the diameter of the hook shaft in millimetres. Before metric sizing, crochet hooks were sized in two ranges: steel hooks (small sizes for fine work) and aluminium or plastic hooks (larger sizes, sometimes called wool hooks). U.S. sizes were used in America and Imperial sizes in the U.K. and Canada, and it is useful to understand these: you may have old hooks in your collection, or wish to follow an old crochet pattern.

You can see from the table opposite how hooks labelled under different systems may be confused. Always measure your own tension.

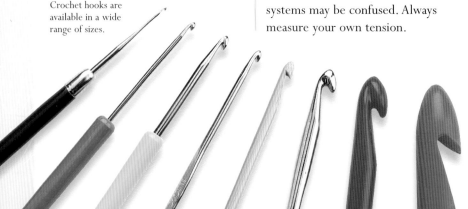

Approximate equivalent hook sizes

For guidance only, sizes given do not necessarily correspond exactly.

International standard range (ISR)	Imperial steel hooks	Imperial aluminium or or plastic hooks	U.S. steel hooks	U.S. aluminium or plastic hooks
0.6mm	6		14	
0.75mm	5		13	
1mm	4		12	
	3½		11	
1.25mm	3		10	
			9	
1.5mm	2½		8	
			7	
1.75mm	2		6	
	1½		5	
2mm	1	14	4	
			3	
2.25mm	1/0 or 0	13	2	B
2.5mm	2/0 or 00	12	1	C
3mm	3/0 or 000	11	0	D
		10		
3.5mm		9	00	E
				F
4mm		8		
				G
4.5mm		7		
5mm		6		H
5.5mm		5		I
6mm		4		J
6.5mm		3		K
7mm		2		L
8mm		1		M
9mm		0		N
10mm				
12mm				
15mm				

Tunisian hooks

These are much longer than a normal hook, with a cylindrical shaft and a knob at the end. Tunisian hooks are available in a wide range of sizes and extra-long hooks have separate sections that screw together. Another name for a Tunisian hook is a "tricot needle".

2

3

4

1

Yarns

1 Yarns sold specifically for crochet are fine, smooth cottons, usually described by a number ranging from 5 (the coarsest) to 60 (very fine yarn used for traditional crochet). These cotton yarns are often described as "mercerised", which means they have been treated with an alkali to improve their strength and lustre. They are ideal for showing off intricate patterns and textures.

2 Fine, natural-linen yarns are also suitable for crochet, and give a crisp finish to the work.

3 Pearl-cotton yarns are sold for use in crochet, knitting and embroidery, and give a softer and less tightly twisted finish than traditional crochet yarns. They are manufactured in a range of thicknesses.

4 Smooth, firm knitting yarns are also suitable for crochet. These are sold in various weights, from 3-ply (the finest) through 4-ply, double knitting and aran weight, to chunky weight. They may be cotton, wool, or synthetic.

TIP

Yarn supplied in hanks must be wound into a ball before you begin to crochet.

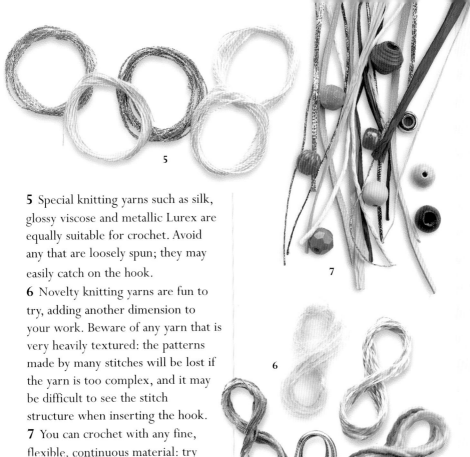

5 Special knitting yarns such as silk, glossy viscose and metallic Lurex are equally suitable for crochet. Avoid any that are loosely spun; they may easily catch on the hook.

6 Novelty knitting yarns are fun to try, adding another dimension to your work. Beware of any yarn that is very heavily textured: the patterns made by many stitches will be lost if the yarn is too complex, and it may be difficult to see the stitch structure when inserting the hook.

7 You can crochet with any fine, flexible, continuous material: try string (natural or synthetic), raffia, or leather thonging. Many novelty threads such as metallic tapes are sold as embroidery materials. Beads for crochet should have holes large enough to thread easily onto the yarn.

TIP

When choosing an unfamiliar yarn, it is a good idea to buy just one ball and experiment with it before purchasing all the yarn for a large project.

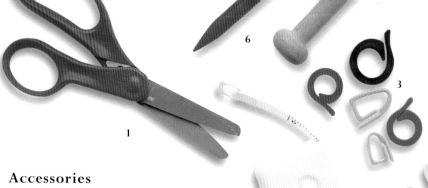

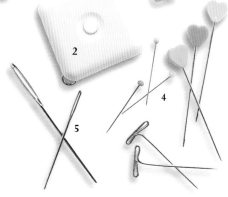

Accessories

Only a few accessories are needed to complete a crochet project.

1 Small, sharp scissors for cutting yarn.

2 A tape measure for checking your tension (see page 42).

3 Split ring markers are slipped onto a particular stitch or row, as an aid to counting. They may also be used as stitch holders, especially when working with several colours; the loop from the hook is slipped onto a ring to secure it while you are working another part of the pattern in a different colour.

4 To hold your work during assembly, choose pins with large heads that will not disappear between the stitches.

5 Tapestry needles are the best type to use for sewing seams. They have a large eye and a blunt tip that will not split the yarn, and are available in a range of sizes.

6 If you want to try any of the broomstick lace patterns (see pages 232–235), you will also need one large knitting needle of around size 15mm). These are available in wood or plastic. A needle with a tip that tapers sharply over a short distance is easier to use than one with a long, gradual taper.

TIP

If you need a larger rod for broomstick crochet, sharpen one end of a wooden dowel rod and smooth it carefully with sandpaper before use.

How to Begin

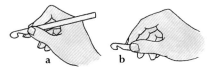

Holding the hook

The hook is held in the right hand (if you are right-handed). There are two ways to hold a crochet hook: like a pencil (a) or like a knife (b). The hook should face downward.

Making a slip knot

Almost every piece of crochet begins with a slip knot.

Step 1: Loop the yarn in the direction shown, insert the hook through the loop to catch the yarn leading to the ball (not the short tail), and pull it through to make a loop.

Step 2: Pull gently on both yarn ends to tighten the knot against the hook.

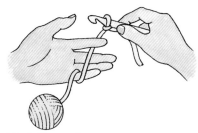

Holding the yarn

The left hand (if you are right-handed) controls the supply of yarn. It is important to maintain an even tension on the yarn. One method is to wind the yarn around the fingers, as shown above.

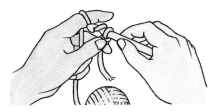

To form a stitch use the first finger to bring the yarn into position so it may be caught by the hook and pulled through to make a new loop. Note the direction of the yarn around the tip of the hook.

TIP

If you are left-handed, hold the hook in your left hand and the yarn in your right, and look at the reflection of these illustrations in a mirror.

Basic Stitches
and their abbreviations and symbols

Chain stitch (CH or ch)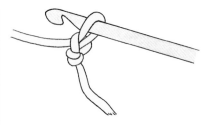

Most pieces of crochet begin with a foundation chain of a certain number of stitches. Chains worked at the beginning of a row, or as part of a stitch pattern, are worked in the same way as below.

Step 2: Pull a new loop through the loop on the hook. 1 CH made.

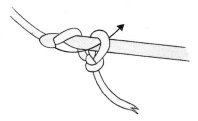

Step 1: Hold the yarn and slip knot as shown on page 15. Wrap the yarn around the hook in the direction shown (or catch it with the hook).

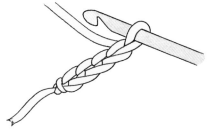

Step 3: Repeat steps 1 and 2 as required, moving your left hand every few stitches to hold the chain just below the hook. Tighten the slip knot by pulling on the short yarn tail.

TIP

Making the correct number of foundation chains is crucial when working a pattern. Count the chains as you make them, and count them again before continuing. Do not count the slip knot as a chain.

Slip stitch (SS or ss)   •

Step 1: Begin with a length of chains. Insert the hook in the second chain from the hook, wrap the yarn around the hook, and pull a new loop through both the work and the loop on the hook. 1 SS made.

Step 2: Repeat step 1 in each chain to the end. 1 row of SS made.

TIP

When working into a foundation chain, you can insert the hook under either one or two threads of each chain, as you prefer, but be consistent. For a firm edge, insert under two threads; for a looser edge, insert under one thread.

Double crochet (DC or dc)   +

Step 1: Begin with a length of chains. Insert the hook in the second chain from the hook, wrap the yarn around the hook, and pull the new loop through the chain only.

Step 2: Wrap the yarn around the hook, and pull a loop through both loops on the hook.

Step 3: One loop remains on the hook. 1 DC made. Repeat steps 1 and 2 in each chain to the end. 1 row of DC made.

Extended double crochet
(EXDC or exdc)

Step 1: Begin with a length of chains. Insert the hook in the third chain from the hook, wrap the yarn around the hook, and pull the new loop through the chain.

Step 2: Wrap the yarn around the hook, and pull it through the first loop only.

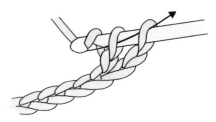

Step 3: You now have two loops on the hook. Wrap the yarn again, and pull it through both loops.

Step 4: One loop remains on the hook. 1 EXDC made. Repeat steps 1 through 3 in each chain to the end. 1 row of EXDC made.

TIP

For any stitch, the yarn is always wrapped around the hook in the direction shown, unless specific instructions direct otherwise.

Half treble (HTR or htr)

Step 1: Begin with a length of chains. Wrap the yarn around the hook, and insert the hook in the third chain from the hook.

Step 2: Pull a loop through this chain. You now have three loops on the hook. Wrap the yarn around the hook again. Pull through all three loops on the hook.

Step 3: One loop remains on the hook. 1 HTR made. Repeat steps 1 through 3 in each chain to the end. 1 row of HTR made.

Treble (TR or tr)

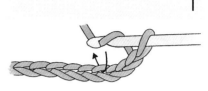

Step 1: Begin with a length of chains. Wrap the yarn around the hook, and insert the hook in the fourth chain from the hook.

Step 2: Pull a loop through this chain to make three loops on the hook. Wrap the yarn around the hook again. Pull a new loop through the first two loops on the hook. Two loops remain on the hook. Wrap the yarn around the hook again. Pull a new loop through both loops on the hook.

Step 3: 1 TR made. Repeat steps 1 through 3 in each chain to the end. 1 row of TR made.

Double treble (DTR or dtr)

Step 1: Begin with a length of chains. Wrap the yarn twice around the hook, and insert the hook in the fifth chain from the hook.

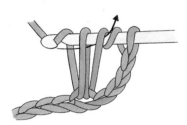

Step 2: Pull a loop through this chain. You now have four loops on the hook. Wrap the yarn again and pull through the first two loops.

TIP

Make triple trebles or quadruple trebles in a similar way. Wrap the yarn three (or four) times around the hook, insert the hook, pull a loop through, then * wrap the yarn around the hook, pull a loop through the first two loops, and repeat from * until one loop remains.

Step 3: Three loops remain on the hook. Wrap the yarn around the hook and pull through the first two loops.

Step 4: Two loops remain on the hook. Wrap the yarn again and pull through the two remaining loops.

Step 5: 1 DTR made. Repeat steps 1 through 5 in each chain to the end. 1 row of DTR made.

Crochet Essentials

Basic Techniques

Working in rows

The basic stitches described may be repeated in rows to make simple textured fabrics, as shown on pages 54–58.

When you work the first row onto the foundation chain, you begin the first stitch in the second, third, fourth, or fifth chain from the hook, depending on the height of the stitch you are making; the one, two, three, or four chains that you skip stand instead of the first stitch of the first row. Every following row begins with a similar number of chains, called the turning chain(s). The next examples show rows of trebles, with three turning chains.

More complicated stitch patterns usually follow the same principle.

Turning the work

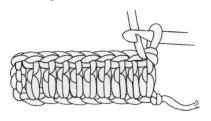

Step 1: When the first row is complete, turn the work. You can turn it either clockwise or anti-clockwise, but a neater edge will result if you are consistent.

At the beginning of the next row, work a number of turning chains to correspond with the stitch in use, as below. These chains will stand for the first stitch of the new row, and are counted as one stitch.

Table of Turning Chains	
double crochet	1 chain
extended double crochet	2 chains
half treble	2 chains
treble	3 chains
double treble	4 chains
triple treble	5 chains

NOTE: These are the usual numbers of turning chains used for the basic stitches. Sometimes two chains are needed for double crochet, and the requirements of more complicated stitch patterns may vary.

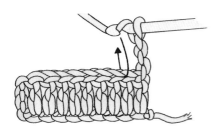

Step 2: Work the appropriate number of chains (three are shown here). Skip the last stitch of the previous row and work into the next stitch. The hook is normally inserted under the top two threads of each stitch, as shown. (When the hook is to be inserted elsewhere, pattern instructions will indicate this.)

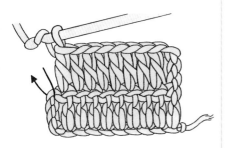

Step 3: At the end of the row, work the last stitch into the top of the chains at the beginning of the previous row. Then repeat steps 1 through 3.

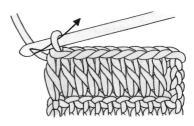

Fastening off
To fasten off the yarn securely, work one chain, then cut the yarn at least 4 in. (10cm) away from the work, and pull the tail through the loop on the hook, tightening it gently.

Joining in a new yarn

Sometimes yarn is fastened off in one position and then rejoined elsewhere (to work an edging, for example). Also if your first ball of yarn runs out, you will have to join in another.

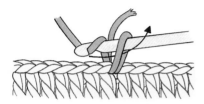

Insert the hook as required, wrap the yarn over it, and pull a loop through. Leave a tail of about 4 in. (10cm). Work one chain, and continue the pattern. If you are using a solid stitch work the next few stitches for about 2 in. (5 cm) enclosing the yarn tail, then pull gently on the tail and snip off the excess.

TIP

Try to avoid running out of yarn in the middle of a row. When you think you have enough yarn left for *two* rows, tie a loose overhand knot at the centre of the remaining yarn. Work one row. If you need to undo the knot, there is not enough yarn left for another complete row. Fasten off the old ball at the side edge and use a new ball for the next row.

Changing colours

Use this method for a neat join between colours. The first ball need not be fastened off: it may be left aside for a few rows or stitches in the course of a multi-coloured pattern.

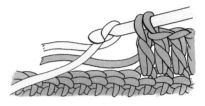

Step 1: Work up to the final "yrh, pull through" of the last stitch in the old colour and wrap the new colour around the hook.

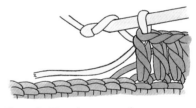

Step 2: Use the new colour to complete the stitch.

Step 3: Continue in the new colour.

Seams

Crochet pieces may be seamed either by sewing them with a tapestry needle or by crocheting them together with a hook. In either case, use the same yarn as used for the main pieces, if possible. If this is too bulky, choose a matching, finer yarn, preferably with the same fibre content to avoid problems when the article is washed.

Woven seam

This seam is flexible and flat, making it suitable for fine work and for baby clothes. Lay the pieces with edges touching, wrong sides up, and use a tapestry needle and matching yarn to weave around the centres of the edge stitches, as shown. Do not pull the stitches too tightly: the seam should stretch as much as the work itself. When joining row ends, work in a similar way.

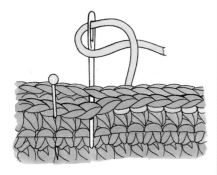

Back stitch seam

A firm seam that resists stretching, used for hard-wearing garments and articles such as bags, and for areas where firmness is an advantage, such as the shoulder seams of a garment.

Hold the pieces with right sides together (pin them if necessary, as shown), matching the stitches or row ends, and use a tapestry needle and matching yarn to work backstitches, as shown.

TIP

When fastening off, leave longer tails where they will be useful for sewing seams.

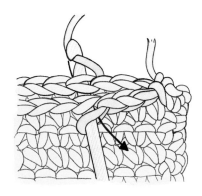

When working this seam along side edges, match the row ends carefully. Make a suitable number of slip stitches to the side edge of each row so that the seam is not too tight: for example, two or three slip stitches along the side edge of each row of trebles.

Slip stitch seam

This seam may be worked with right sides together, so that the seam is inside, or with wrong sides together, so that the seam shows as a ridge on the right side of the work. Insert the hook through the corresponding stitches of each edge to work one slip stitch (see page 17) through each pair of stitches along the seam. Fasten off securely.

You can insert the hook under two threads of each stitch, as shown here; alternatively, for a less bulky seam, insert the hook under the back loop only of the nearer edge and the front loop only of the further edge.

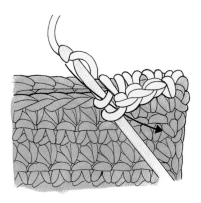

Double crochet seam

Again, this seam may be worked with wrong or right sides together, so that it appears on the inside or outside of the article. Work as for the slip stitch seam, but in double crochet (see page 17).

Working in rounds

Crochet may be worked in rounds instead of rows. If a flat circle is required, it is necessary to increase the number of stitches on every round (see Circle in Trebles, page 213). If the increases are grouped together to make corners, then a triangle, square, hexagon, or other flat shape will result (see pages 215–219). If no increasing is worked, the crochet will form a tube.

Chain ring

This is the usual way to begin when working in rounds. The chain ring may be any size, as required, leaving a small or large hole at the centre of the work.

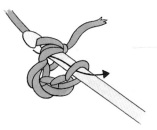

Make the number of chains required. Without twisting the chains, join them into a ring with a slip stitch into the first chain made.

Work a round

Step 1: Each round usually begins with a number of starting chains, to stand for the first stitch. Here, three starting chains stand for the first treble. The first round is usually worked by inserting the hook in the centre of the chain ring.

Step 2: To join the round at the end, work a slip stitch into the last starting chain made.

On the following rounds, insert the hook in the normal way under two threads at the top of each stitch, unless directed otherwise.

Fastening off

Step 1: To fasten off when working in rounds, work the slip stitch joining the last round, then cut the yarn leaving a short tail, and draw the tail through the slip stitch.

Step 2: Reinsert the hook from the back, in the position where the slip stitch was worked, catch the yarn tail, and pull it through to the back of the work.

TIP

For a shape with a closed centre, work the first round of stitches over the tail of yarn as well as the chain ring. Then pull gently on the tail to draw the centre together.

Finger wrap Ω

Used for a tight centre with no visible hole.

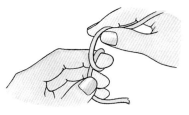

Step 1: Wrap the yarn once (or two or three times) around your finger.

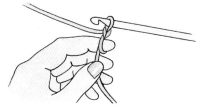

Step 2: Work the first stitch into the loop, as shown.

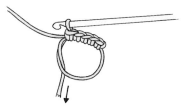

Step 3: Slip the loop off your finger and work the first round into it. (double crochet shown). Pull gently on the yarn tail to tighten the centre.

Joining shapes with picots

Squares and other shapes with picots at the edges may be joined at the tips of the picots.

Work the first square completely, then join on the second square as follows:

Step 1: Work the last round of the second square up to the third corner picot.

TIPS

• Shapes that are edged with arcs of chain stitch may be joined together in a similar way, linking the stitches at the centres of corresponding arcs.

• Shapes may also be joined at the top of any pair of corresponding stitches. Complete a stitch on the final round of the second shape, and work a slip stitch in the top of the corresponding stitch on the first shape before continuing.

Step 2: Work the corner picot up to the centre chain (if five chains are required, for example, work two). Then insert the hook from the back through the centre of the corresponding picot of the first square, work one chain, then work the remaining chains (in this example, two) and complete the picot. Work each picot along this side of the square in the same way, and complete the second square. Subsequent squares may be joined on in a similar way as you complete them, on one or more sides.

Stitch Variations

Basic stitches may be varied in many ways, for example, by working several stitches in the same place, by inserting the hook in a different place, by working several stitches together, or by working in the reverse direction. Some special stitches are worked with the help of a rod to make long loops. In surface crochet, chain stitches are overlaid onto a crochet background.

Here, five trebles are shown worked into the same foundation chain, making a shell.

Working several stitches in the same place

Increasing
This technique is used to increase the total number of stitches when shaping a garment or other item. Increases may be worked at the edges of flat pieces, or at any point along a row or round.

Patterning
Two, three, or more stitches may be worked into the same place to make a fan of stitches, often called a shell. The total number of stitches is increased, so when working a stitch pattern other stitches are worked together or skipped to compensate.

Working into one loop
If the hook is inserted under just one loop at the top of a stitch, the empty loop creates a ridge on either the front or the back of the fabric.

Front loop only

If the hook is inserted under the front loop only, the empty back loop will show as a ridge on the other side of the work.

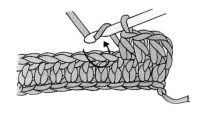

Back loop only

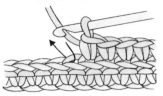

If the hook is inserted under the back loop only, the empty front loop creates a ridge on the side of the work facing you. This example shows double crochet.

NOTE: In this book, "front loop" means the loop nearest to you, at the top of the stitch, and "back loop" means the farther loop, whether you are working a right-side or a wrong-side row.

Into a chain space

The hook is inserted into the space below one or more chains. Here, a treble is being worked into a one chain space.

Inserting between stitches

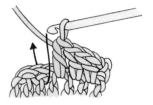

The hook is inserted between the stitches of the previous row, instead of at the top of a stitch.

Spike stitches

Many pattern variations may be made by inserting the hook one or more rows below the previous row. The insertion may be directly below the next stitch, or one or more stitches to the right or left.

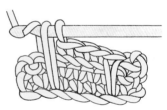

Insert the hook as directed, wrap the yarn around the hook, and pull the loop through the work, lengthening the loop to the height of the working row. Complete the stitch as instructed. (Double crochet spike shown here.)

Raised stitches

These are created by inserting the hook around the stem of the stitch below, from the front or the back.

These two examples show raised trebles, but shorter or longer stitches may be worked in a similar way:

Front raised treble (FRTR or frtr) (raised treble front)

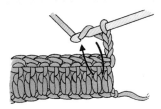

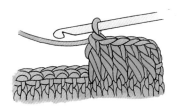

Step 1: Wrap the yarn around the hook, insert the hook from the front to the back at right of the next stitch, and bring it out at left of the same stitch. The hook is now round the stem of the stitch.

Step 2: Complete the treble in the usual way. A ridge forms on the other side of the work.

Back raised treble (BRTR or brtr) (raised treble back)

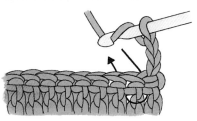

Step 1: Wrap the yarn around the hook, insert the hook from the back through to the front at right of the next stitch, and through to the back again at left of the same stitch.

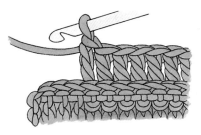

Step 2: Complete the treble in the usual way. A ridge forms on the side of the work facing you.

Working several stitches together

Decreasing

Two or more stitches may be joined together at the top to decrease the total number of stitches when shaping the work, using the same method as for clusters, below.

Patterning

Joining groups of stitches together makes several decorative stitch formations: clusters, puffs, bobbles and popcorns.

Cluster (CL or cl)

A cluster is a group of stitches, joined closely together at the top. (Sometimes the term is also used for groups joined at both top and bottom.)

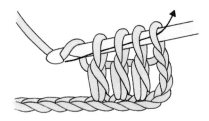

Step 1: Work each of the stitches to be joined up to the last "yrh, pull through" that will complete it. One loop from each stitch to be joined should remain on the hook, plus the loop from the previous stitch. Wrap the yarn around the hook once again.

Step 2: Pull a loop through all the loops on the hook. One loop now remains on the hook. Three trebles are shown here worked together, but any number of any type of stitch may be worked together in a similar way.

Puff (PS or ps)

A puff is normally a group of three or more half trebles, joined at both top and bottom (a three-half-treble puff is shown below).

Step 1: * Wrap the yarn around the hook, insert the hook where required, draw through a loop, repeat from * two (or more) times in the same place. You now have seven loops (or more) on the hook. Wrap the yarn round the hook again, and pull through all the loops on the hook.

Step 2: Often, one chain is worked to close the puff.

Bobble

A bobble is usually a group of several trebles (or longer stitches) joined at both top and bottom. It is often surrounded by shorter stitches, and worked on a wrong-side row (a three-treble bobble is shown here).

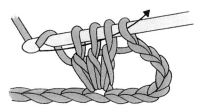

Step 1: * Wrap the yarn around the hook, insert the hook where required, pull a loop through, wrap the yarn around the hook, pull through the first two loops, repeat from * two (or more) times in the same place. Wrap the yarn around the hook, and pull through all loops.

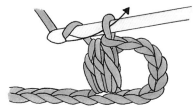

Step 2: Work one chain to close.

Popcorn (PC or pc)

A popcorn is formed when several complete trebles (or longer stitches) are worked in the same place, and the top of the first stitch is joined to the last to make a "cup" shape. A four-treble popcorn is shown below.

Step 1: Work four trebles (or number required) in the same place.

Step 2: Slip the last loop off the hook. Reinsert the hook in the top of the first treble of the group, as shown, and catch the empty loop. (On a wrong-side row, reinsert the hook from the back, to push the popcorn to the right side of the work.)

Step 3: Pull this loop through to close the top of the popcorn.

TIP

Sometimes the closing stitch of a popcorn is worked through the back loop only of the first stitch of the group and sometimes through the stitch made just before the group.

Special formations

Picot

Formed by three or more chains closed into a ring with a slip stitch (or a double crochet).

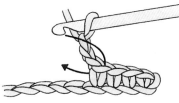

Step 1: Work three chains (or number required). Insert the hook as instructed. The arrow shows how to insert the hook down through the top of the previous double crochet.

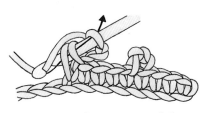

Step 2: Wrap the yarn around the hook and pull through all the loops to close the picot with a slip stitch.

Bullion stitch (BS or bs)

A bullion stitch is formed by wrapping the yarn several times (normally seven to ten) around the hook, and pulling a loop through.

Step 1: Wrap the yarn (not too tightly) as many times as directed around the hook. Insert the hook where required, and pull through a loop. Wrap the yarn around the hook again.

Step 2: Pull through all the loops on the hook. You can ease each loop in turn off the hook, rather than try to pull through all of them at once.

Working in the reverse direction

Reverse double crochet (corded double crochet, crab stitch)
(REV DC or rev dc)

Usually used as an edging and worked from left to right, giving an extra twist to each stitch.

Step 1: After completing a right-side row, do not turn the work. Insert the hook in the first stitch to the right, turning the hook downward to catch the yarn and pull it through.

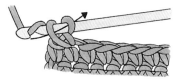

Step 2: Catch the yarn again, and pull it through both loops on the hook to complete the stitch. Repeat Steps 1 and 2 to the right.

Lengthening stitch loops

Broomstick-loop stitch
(LS or ls)

Use a rod such as a large knitting needle. The loops are shown here worked into a foundation chain, but may be worked into other stitches in the same way.

Step 1: Work from left to right. Hold the rod in your left hand. Insert the hook as directed, wrap the yarn around the hook, and pull through a loop. Lengthen this loop, and insert the tip of the rod in the direction indicated by the arrow. Push the loop down the rod. Repeat as required.

Step 2: A row of loops may be worked on the next row in various ways. Here, five loops are worked together.

Bouclé loop stitch
(fur stitch) (BLS or bls) Ⴑ

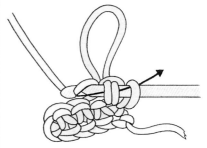

This stitch is normally worked on a wrong-side row, forming a line of loops on the right side of the work. It may be worked as a single row, to form a fringe, or repeated as on page 230.

Step 2: Wrap the yarn around the hook again, and pull it through all the loops on the hook.

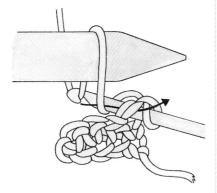

Step 1: Insert the hook in the usual way, wrap the yarn around the rod as shown, and catch both threads below the rod with the hook to pull them through the work.

Step 3: The loop is now firmly anchored. Repeat to the left as required.

TIP
If preferred, you can use your left forefinger instead of a rod to make the loops, but it takes practice to keep the loops all the same length.

Solomon's knot (SK or sk)

A Solomon's knot (see pages 91–92)
is simply a lengthened chain stitch,
locked in place with a double crochet
in the back loop, as below.

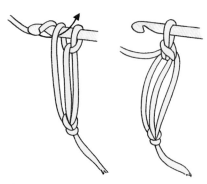

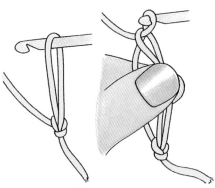

Step 3: Insert
the hook under
this separate
thread, wrap the
yarn around the
hook, and pull
through the first
loop.

Step 4: Wrap
the yarn around
the hook again
and pull through
both loops to
complete the
knot.

Step 1: Work
one chain, and
lengthen it as
required:
normally about
⅜ to ⅝ in.
(10–15mm).

Step 2: Wrap
the yarn around
the hook and
pull through,
keeping this loop
to a normal size.
Hold the
lengthened first
chain separate
from the thread
leading to the
new loop.

Locking stitch (LKS or lks)

Use steps 2 to 4 to lock any long
loop, securing it to length, as in the
broomstick-crochet patterns on pages
231–235.

Variation on the foundation chain

Double foundation chain

This foundation chain is more elastic than a single chain, and easier to count.

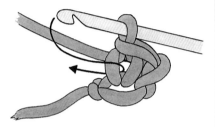

Step 1: Make two chains. Work one double crochet in the first chain made.

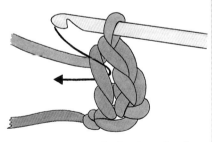

Step 2: Inserting the hook under the left-hand thread of the last double crochet made, work another double crochet. Repeat step 2 as required.

Surface crochet

Overlaid chain (OCH or och)

Overlaid chain patterns, known as surface crochet, may be added to Small Mesh Ground (page 86) or Large Mesh Ground (page 87), or used to decorate any plain fabric such as double or treble crochet.

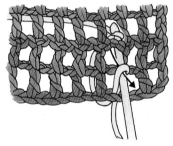

Step 1: Hold the yarn at the back of the work. Insert the hook through the crochet fabric as required, catch a loop, and pull it through. You now have one loop on the hook. Insert the hook through the fabric again, as required, catch the yarn, and pull the loop through both the work and the loop on the hook. One OCH made.

Tunisian Stitches

Tunisian crochet is worked in rows, but without turning the work. On "forward" rows, worked from right to left, all the loops made are kept on the hook. On "reverse" rows, from left to right, the loops are worked off in turn. A Tunisian hook, or "tricot needle" (page 11), is required for work of any width (but you can try out a few stitches with an ordinary straight-shafted hook).

Tunisian base rows

Most Tunisian work begins with a foundation chain of the required length, followed by these two base rows, equivalent to two rows of Tunisian simple stitch (shown on page 41) and charted with the same symbols.

Forward base row

Step 1: Insert the hook in the second chain from the hook, wrap the yarn around the hook, and pull the loop through.

Step 2: Repeat this stitch in each chain to the end. Do not turn.

Reverse base row

Step 1: Work one chain. *Wrap the yarn around the hook, and pull it through the first two loops on the hook. Repeat from * to end.

Step 2: One loop now remains on the hook. As a rule, this loop stands for the first stitch of the next row, so the next row begins by inserting the hook in the second stitch.

Tunisian simple stitch
(TSS or tss)

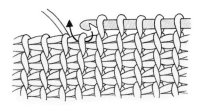

Forward row
Insert the hook under the single vertical thread, from right to left, then wrap the yarn around the hook and pull through, keeping the loop on the hook. Repeat as required.

Reverse row
As reverse base row.

Tunisian knit stitch
(TKS or tks)

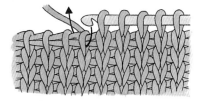

Forward row
Insert the hook through the centre of the stitch below, from front to back, then wrap the yarn around the hook and pull through, keeping the loop on the hook. Repeat as required.

Reverse row
As reverse base row.

Tunisian purl stitch
(TPS or tps)

Forward row
Bring the yarn forward to the front of the work. Insert the hook under a single vertical thread in the same way as for Tunisian simple stitch, then take the yarn to the back, wrap it around the hook as shown, and pull through, keeping the loop on the hook. Repeat as required.

Reverse row
As reverse base row.

Measuring Tension

Most crochet patterns recommend a "tension". This is the number of stitches (or pattern repeats) and rows to a given measurement (usually 4 in. or 10cm). For your work to be the correct size, you must match this tension as closely as possible. To work out a design of your own, you need to measure your tension to calculate the stitches and rows required.

The hook size recommended by any pattern or ball band is only a suggestion. Tension depends not only on the hook and yarn but also on personal technique.

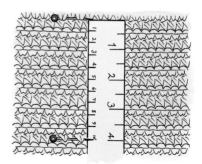

Step 2: Then place two pins 4 in. (10cm) apart on a vertical pattern line near the centre, and count the number of rows between them.

If you have too many stitches (or pattern repeats) or rows to 4 in. (10cm), your work is too tight; repeat the process with another sample made with a larger hook. If you have too few stitches (or pattern repeats), or rows, your work is too loose; try a smaller hook. It is usually more important to match the number of stitches exactly, rather than the number of rows.

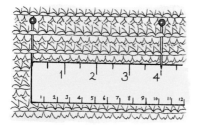

Step 1: Work a piece of crochet about 6 in. (15cm) square, using the hook, yarn, and stitch pattern required. Press if this is recommended on the ball band. Lay the sample flat and place two pins 4 in. (10cm) apart along the same row, near the centre. Count the stitches (or pattern repeats) between them.

Blocking Crochet

Crochet often needs to be blocked before assembly, to "set" the stitches and give a professional finish.

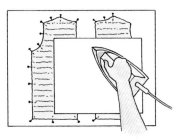

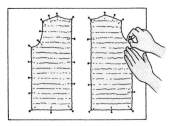

Step 1: Lay each piece right side down on a well-padded surface. With rows straight, pin the pieces in place, inserting pins evenly all around at right angles to the edges. If necessary, ease the piece gently to size, checking the measurements. (Matching pieces, such as the two garment fronts shown here, may be pinned out side by side).

Step 2: Check the yarn band for pressing instructions. For natural fibres, such as wool or cotton, a clean damp cloth and a warm iron are usually suitable. Lift and replace the iron lightly, do not rub. Leave to cool and dry completely before removing the pins. After assembly, press the seams gently.

TIP

Some yarns (such as some synthetics) should not be pressed: pin out the work as above, mist with water, and leave to dry.

Crochet Aftercare

It is a good idea to keep a ball band from each project you complete as a reference for washing instructions. Crochet items are best washed gently by hand and dried flat, to keep their shape. Crochet garments should not be hung on coat hangers, but folded and stored flat, away from dust, damp, heat, and sunlight. Clean tissue paper is better than a plastic bag.

Stitch Selector

*All the stitches used in this book are displayed over the next few pages. Use the
page references to take you to the relevant instructions for each stitch.*

Basic Stitch Patterns

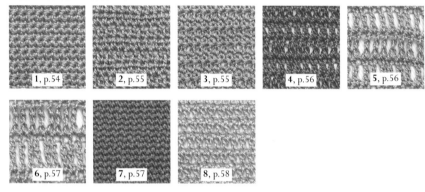

1, p.54
2, p.55
3, p.55
4, p.56
5, p.56
6, p.57
7, p.57
8, p.58

Textured Stitches

9, p.59
10, p.60
11, p.60
12, p.61
13, p.61
14, p.62
15, p.62
16, p.63
17, p.63
18, p.64
19, p.64
20, p.65
21, p.65
22, p.66
23, p.66

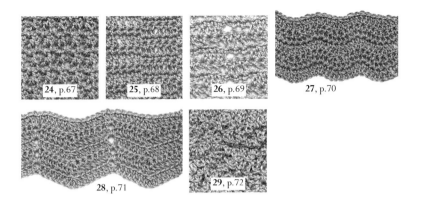

24, p.67
25, p.68
26, p.69
27, p.70
28, p.71
29, p.72

Fans and Shells

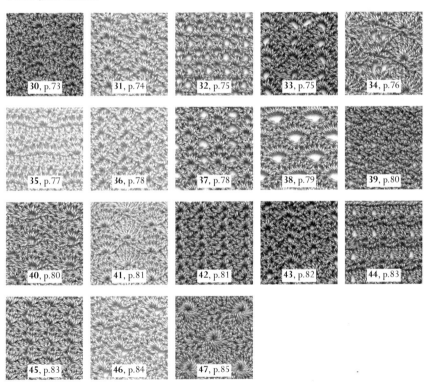

30, p.73
31, p.74
32, p.75
33, p.75
34, p.76
35, p.77
36, p.78
37, p.78
38, p.79
39, p.80
40, p.80
41, p.81
42, p.81
43, p.82
44, p.83
45, p.83
46, p.84
47, p.85

Mesh and Filet Stitches

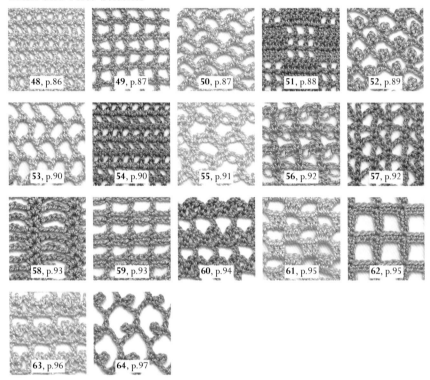

48, p.86
49, p.87
50, p.87
51, p.88
52, p.89
53, p.90
54, p.90
55, p.91
56, p.92
57, p.92
58, p.93
59, p.93
60, p.94
61, p.95
62, p.95
63, p.96
64, p.97

Openwork and Lace Stitches

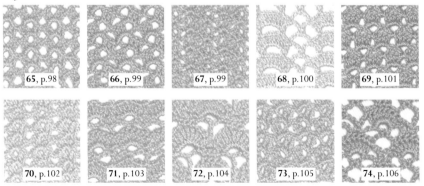

65, p.98
66, p.99
67, p.99
68, p.100
69, p.101
70, p.102
71, p.103
72, p.104
73, p.105
74, p.106

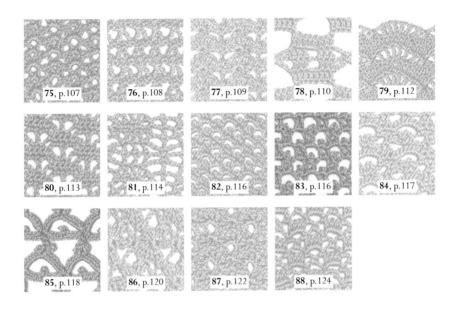

75, p.107 76, p.108 77, p.109 78, p.110 79, p.112

80, p.113 81, p.114 82, p.116 83, p.116 84, p.117

85, p.118 86, p.120 87, p.122 88, p.124

Trims and Edgings

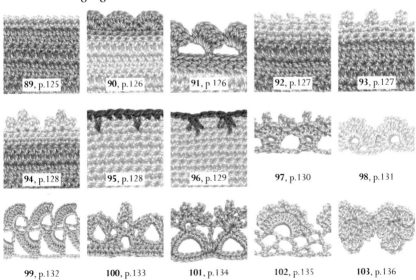

89, p.125 90, p.126 91, p.126 92, p.127 93, p.127

94, p.128 95, p.128 96, p.129 97, p.130 98, p.131

99, p.132 100, p.133 101, p.134 102, p.135 103, p.136

Clusters, Puffs and Bobbles

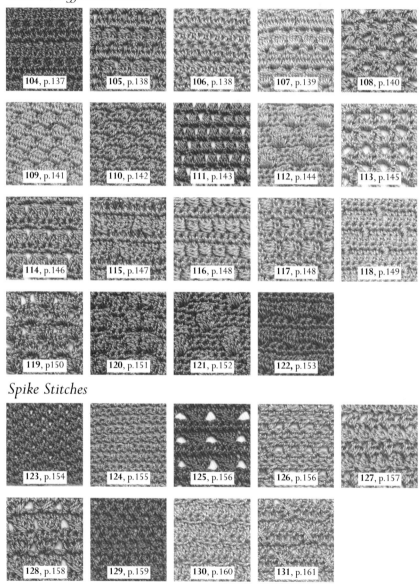

104, p.137

105, p.138

106, p.138

107, p.139

108, p.140

109, p.141

110, p.142

111, p.143

112, p.144

113, p.145

114, p.146

115, p.147

116, p.148

117, p.148

118, p.149

119, p150

120, p.151

121, p.152

122, p.153

Spike Stitches

123, p.154

124, p.155

125, p.156

126, p.156

127, p.157

128, p.158

129, p.159

130, p.160

131, p.161

Relief Stitches

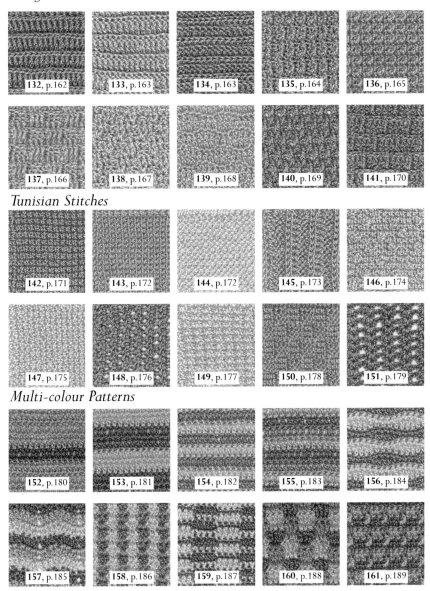

132, p.162 133, p.163 134, p.163 135, p.164 136, p.165

137, p.166 138, p.167 139, p.168 140, p.169 141, p.170

Tunisian Stitches

142, p.171 143, p.172 144, p.172 145, p.173 146, p.174

147, p.175 148, p.176 149, p.177 150, p.178 151, p.179

Multi-colour Patterns

152, p.180 153, p.181 154, p.182 155, p.183 156, p.184

157, p.185 158, p.186 159, p.187 160, p.188 161, p.189

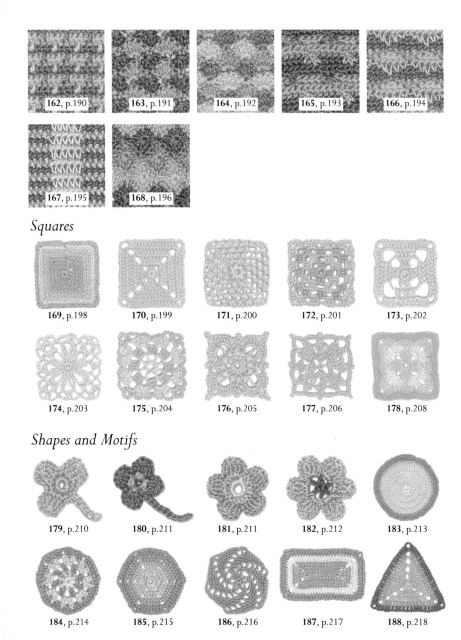

162, p.190   163, p.191   164, p.192   165, p.193   166, p.194

167, p.195   168, p.196

Squares

169, p.198   170, p.199   171, p.200   172, p.201   173, p.202

174, p.203   175, p.204   176, p.205   177, p.206   178, p.208

Shapes and Motifs

179, p.210   180, p.211   181, p.211   182, p.212   183, p.213

184, p.214   185, p.215   186, p.216   187, p.217   188, p.218

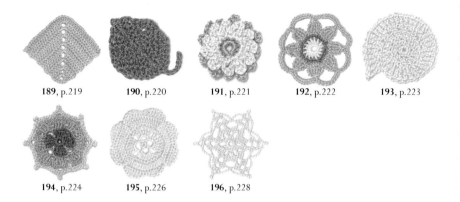

189, p.219 190, p.220 191, p.221 192, p.222 193, p.223

194, p.224 195, p.226 196, p.228

Special Stitches

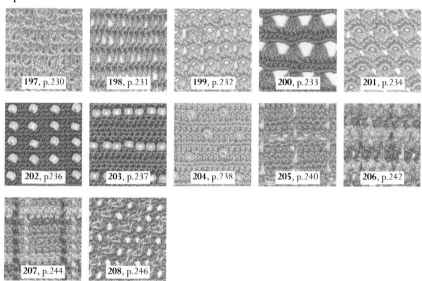

197, p.230 198, p.231 199, p.232 200, p.233 201, p.234

202, p236 203, p.237 204, p.238 205, p.240 206, p.242

207, p.244 208, p.246

The
Stitch Collection

The stitch patterns are organised into fourteen types, from basic stitches through to special techniques. Try a small sample of any stitch using a plain yarn in a light colour to help you understand the construction.

1

Basic Stitch Patterns

The simplest crochet stitches, worked in repeat, form closely textured patterns that are easy and quick to make. Double crochet and half treble rows both make firm, stable fabrics; longer stitches (such as trebles) are more flexible.

Double crochet rows

Any number of sts.

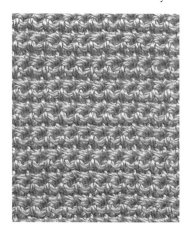

Row 1: 1 DC in 2nd ch from hook, 1 DC in each ch to end, turn.
Row 2: 1 CH, skip first dc, 1 DC in each dc, ending 1 DC in 1 ch, turn.
Repeat row 2.

Half treble rows

Any number of sts (add 1 for foundation ch).

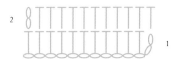

Row 1: 1 HTR in 3rd ch from hook, 1 HTR in each ch to end, turn.
Row 2: 2 CH, skip first htr, 1 HTR in each htr, ending 1 HTR in 2nd of 2 ch, turn.
Repeat row 2.

Extended double crochet rows

Any number of sts (add 1 for foundation ch).

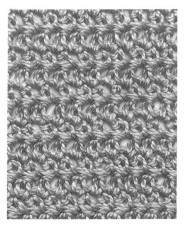

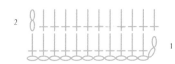

Row 1: 1 EXDC in 3rd ch from hook, 1 EXDC in each ch to end, turn.
Row 2: 2 CH, skip first exdc, 1 EXDC in each exdc, ending 1 EXDC in 2nd of 2 ch, turn.
Repeat row 2.

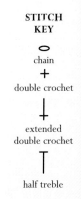

STITCH KEY

o
chain

+
double crochet

extended
double crochet

half treble

Treble rows

Any number of sts (add 2 for
foundation ch).

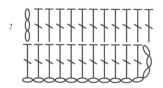

Row 1: 1 TR in 4th ch from
hook (3 skipped ch stand for
first st), 1 TR in each ch to end,
turn.
Row 2: 3 CH (to stand for first
st), skip first tr, 1 TR in each tr,
ending 1 TR in 3rd of 3 ch,
turn.
Repeat row 2.

Double treble

Any number of sts (add 3 for
foundation ch).

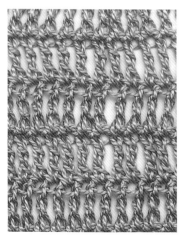

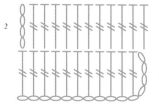

Row 1: 1 DTR in 5th ch from
hook (4 skipped ch stand for
first st), 1 DTR in each ch to
end, turn.
Row 2: 4 CH (to stand for first
st), skip first dtr, 1 DTR in each
dtr, ending 1 DTR in 4th of 4
ch, turn.
Repeat row 2.

Triple treble rows

Any number of sts (add 4 for foundation ch).

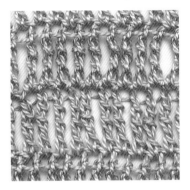

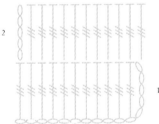

Row 1: 1 TRTR in 6th ch from hook (5 skipped ch stand for first st), 1 TRTR in each ch to end, turn.
Row 2: 5 CH (to stand for first st), skip first trtr, 1 TRTR in each trtr, ending 1 TRTR in 5th of 5 ch, turn.
Repeat row 2.

Double crochet rounds

Worked in rounds without increasing, double crochet makes a firm tube.
Any number of sts (less 1 for foundation ch).

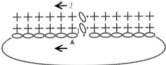

Join into a circle

Make number of CH required and join into a circle with 1 SS in first ch made, without twisting the ch.
Round 1: 1 CH (to stand for first st), 1 DC in first foundation ch made, 1 DC in each ch to end, skip 1 ss, 1 SS under 1 ch at beginning of this round.
Round 2: 1 CH, 1 DC in first dc of previous round, 1 DC in each dc to end, skip 1 ss, 1 SS under 1 ch at beginning of this round.
Repeat round 2.

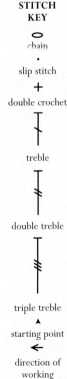

STITCH KEY

○ chain

• slip stitch

+ double crochet

treble

double treble

triple treble

▲ starting point

← direction of working

Treble rounds

Trebles worked in rounds without increasing
make a more flexible tube.
Any number of sts (less 1 for foundation ch).

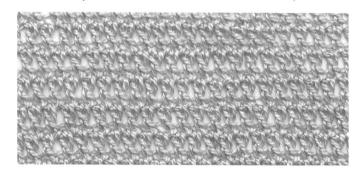

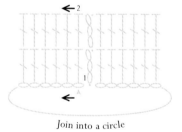

Join into a circle

Make number of CH required and
join into a circle with 1 SS in first
ch made, without twisting the ch.
Round 1: 3 CH (to stand for
first st), 1 TR in first foundation
ch made, 1 TR in each ch to end,
skip 1 ss, 1 SS in 3rd of 3 ch at
beginning of this round.
Round 2: 3 CH, 1 TR in first tr
of previous round, 1 TR in each tr
to end, skip 1 ss, 1 SS in 3rd of 3
ch at beginning of this round.
Repeat round 2.

TIP

Other basic stitches, such as half trebles, double trebles, or triple trebles,
may be used to make tubes. Work in rounds in a similar way, working the
appropriate number of chains at the beginning of each round to stand for the
first stitch (i.e. 2 chains for half trebles, 4 chains for double trebles, 5 chains
for triple trebles).

The Stitch Collection

Textured Stitches 2

Easy variations on the basic stitches produce a wide range of effects. Small, crunchy textures will show to their best advantage worked in smooth yarns, while bolder effects such as ridges or chevrons will suit almost any yarn.

Front loop double crochet

Any number of sts.

Row 1: 1 DC in 2nd ch from hook, 1 DC in each ch to end, turn.
Row 2: 1 CH, skip first dc, 1 DC in front loop of each dc, ending 1 DC in 1 ch, turn.
Repeat row 2.

Back loop double crochet

Any number of sts.

Row 1: 1 DC in 2nd ch from hook, 1 DC in each ch to end, turn.
Row 2: 1 CH, skip first dc, 1 DC in back loop of each dc, ending 1 DC in 1 ch, turn. Repeat row 2.

Front and back loop double crochet

Any number of sts.

Row 1: 1 DC in 2nd ch from hook, 1 DC in each ch to end, turn.
Row 2: 1 CH, skip first dc, 1 DC in front loop of each dc, ending 1 DC in 1 ch, turn.
Row 3: 1 CH, skip first dc, 1 DC in back loop of each dc, ending 1 DC in 1 ch, turn. Repeat rows 2 and 3.

TIP

Whether you are working a right or wrong side row, the front loop is the top thread nearest to you, and the back loop is the top thread furthest away from you (see page 29).

Front loop treble crochet

Any number of sts (add 2 for foundation ch).

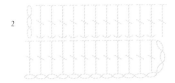

Row 1: 1 TR in 4th ch from hook, 1 TR in each ch to end, turn.
Row 2: 3 CH, skip first tr, 1 TR in front loop of each tr, ending 1 TR in 3rd of 3 ch, turn.
Repeat row 2.

Back loop treble crochet

Any number of sts (add 2 for foundation ch).

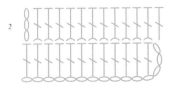

Row 1: 1 TR in 4th ch from hook, 1 TR in each ch to end, turn.
Row 2: 3 CH, skip first tr, 1 TR in back loop of each tr, ending 1 TR in 3rd of 3 ch, turn.
Repeat row 2.

STITCH KEY

◯
chain

+
double crochet

treble

treble in front loop only (see pages 29–30)

treble in back loop only

double crochet in back loop only

double crochet in front loop only

Front and back loop treble crochet

Any number of sts (add 2 for foundation ch).

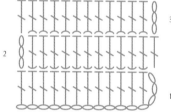

Row 1: 1 TR in 4th ch from hook, 1 TR in each ch to end, turn.

Row 2: 3 CH, skip first tr, 1 TR in front loop of each tr, ending 1 TR in 3rd of 3 ch, turn.

Row 3: 3 CH, skip first tr, 1 TR in back loop of each tr, ending 1 TR in 3rd of 3 ch, turn.

Repeat rows 2 and 3.

Alternate double crochet

Even number of sts.

Row 1: 1 DC in 2nd ch from hook, 1 DC in each ch to end, turn.

Row 2: 1 CH, skip first dc, *1 DC in back loop of next dc, 1 DC in front loop of following dc, repeat from *, ending 1 DC in 1 ch, turn.

Repeat row 2.

Alternate treble crochet

Even number of sts (add 2 for foundation ch).

Row 1: 1 TR in 4th ch from hook (3 skipped ch stand for first st), 1 TR in each ch to end, turn.

Row 2: 3 CH, skip first tr, *1 TR in back loop of next tr, 1 TR in front loop of following tr, repeat from *, ending 1 TR in 3rd of 3 ch, turn.
Repeat row 2.

Paired stitch

Any number of sts (add 1 for foundation ch).

Row 1: 2 DC TOG, inserting hook in 2nd and 3rd ch from hook, *2 DC TOG, inserting hook into same ch as last st, then into next ch, repeat from * to end, turn.

Row 2: 1 CH, 2 DC TOG, inserting hook in first and second 2 dc tog, *2 DC TOG, inserting hook into same place as last st, then into next 2 dc tog, repeat from *, working last insertion in 1 ch, turn.
Repeat row 2.

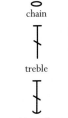

STITCH KEY

○ chain

treble

treble in front loop only

treble in back loop only

+ double crochet

double crochet in front loop only

double crochet in back loop only

✕✕ 2 double crochet together

2

Paired half trebles

Any number of sts (add 2 for foundation ch).

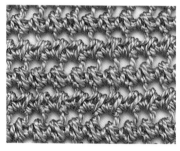

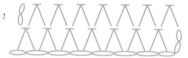

Row 1: 2 HTR TOG, inserting hook in 3rd and 4th ch from hook, *2 HTR TOG, inserting hook in same ch as last st, then in next ch, repeat from * to end, turn.
Row 2: 2 CH, 2 HTR TOG, inserting hook in first and second 2 htr tog, *2 HTR TOG, inserting hook in same place as last st, then in next 2 htr tog, repeat from *, working last insertion in top of 2 ch, turn. Repeat row 2.

Crossed half trebles

Even number of sts (add 1 for foundation ch).

Row 1: 2 HTR TOG, inserting hook in 3rd and 4th ch from hook, *1 CH, 2 HTR TOG, inserting hook in next 2 ch, repeat from * to last ch, 1 CH, 1 HTR in last ch, turn.
Row 2: 2 CH, 2 HTR TOG, inserting hook in first and second ch spaces, *1CH, 2 HTR TOG, inserting hook in same ch sp as last st, then in next ch sp, repeat from *, working last insertion under 2 ch at beginning of previous row, 1 CH, 1 HTR in 2nd of 2 ch, turn. Repeat row 2.

Spider stitch

Odd number of sts (add 2 for foundation ch).

Row 1: [1 DC, 1 CH, 1 DC] in 3rd ch from hook, *skip 1 ch, [1 DC, 1 CH, 1 DC] in next ch, repeat from * to last 2 ch, skip 1 ch, 1 DC in last ch, turn.
Row 2: 2 CH, skip first 2 dc, [1 DC, 1 CH, 1 DC] in each 1 ch sp, ending 1 DC in 2nd of 2 ch, turn.
Repeat row 2.

Up and down stitch

Even number of sts.

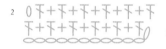

Row 1: 1 TR in 2nd ch from hook, *1 DC in next ch, 1 TR in following ch, repeat from * to end, turn.
Row 2: 1 CH, skip first tr, *1 TR in dc, 1 DC in tr, repeat from * to last st, 1 TR in 1 ch, turn.
Repeat row 2.

STITCH KEY

◦
chain

+ †
double crochet

T
half treble

$\overline{\mathsf{T}}$
treble

$\wedge$

2 half trebles together (see page 19)

Woven stitch

Even number of sts.

Row 1: 1 DC in 2nd ch from hook, *1 CH, skip 1 ch, 1 DC in next ch, repeat from * to end, turn.
Row 2: 1 CH, skip first dc, *1 DC in 1 ch sp, 1 CH, skip 1 dc, repeat from *, ending 1 DC in 1 ch, turn.
Repeat row 2.

Pike stitch

Odd number of sts (add 2 for foundation ch).

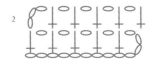

Row 1: 1 EXDC in 5th ch from hook, *1 CH, skip 1 ch, 1 EXDC in next ch, repeat from * to end, turn.
Row 2: 3 CH, skip [1 exdc, 1 ch], *1 EXDC in next exdc, inserting hook to right of single vertical thread, 1 CH, skip 1 ch, repeat from *, ending 1 EXDC in 3rd of 4 ch, turn.
Repeat row 2, working last EXDC in 2nd of 3 ch.

Waffle stitch

Odd number of sts (add 2 for foundation ch).

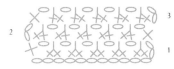

Special stitch – 2 linked EXDC = insert hook as instructed, yrh, pull through a loop, insert hook in next stitch as instructed, yrh, pull through a loop, [yrh, pull through 2 loops] twice.

Row 1: 2 linked EXDC, inserting hook in 3rd and 4th ch from hook, *1 CH, 2 linked EXDC, inserting hook in each of next 2 ch, repeat from *, ending 1 CH, 1 DC in last ch, turn.

Row 2: 2 CH, 2 linked EXDC, inserting hook in first dc and then in next ch sp, *1 CH, 2 linked EXDC, inserting hook to right of next vertical thread (at centre of next exdc) and then in next ch sp, repeat from *, ending 1 CH, 1 DC in last exdc, turn.
Repeat row 2.

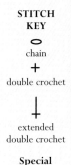

STITCH KEY

o
chain

+
double crochet

↓
extended double crochet

Special Stitches

⋊⋉
2 linked extended double crochet

Wide checkers

A multiple of 10 sts + 5.

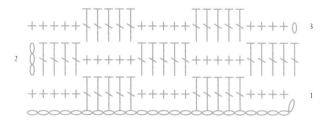

Row 1: 1 DC in 2nd ch from hook, 1 DC in each of next 3 ch, *1 TR in each of next 5 ch, 1 DC in each of following 5 ch, repeat from * to end, turn.
Row 2: 3 CH, skip first dc, 1 TR in each of next 4 dc, *1 DC in each of 5 tr, 1 TR in each of 5 dc, repeat from *, working last TR in 1 ch, turn.

Row 3: 1 CH, skip first tr, 1 DC in each of next 4 tr, *1 TR in each of 5 dc, 1 DC in each of 5 tr, repeat from *, working last DC in 3rd of 3 ch, turn.
Repeat rows 2 and 3.

Wavy checkers

A multiple of 6 sts + 3.

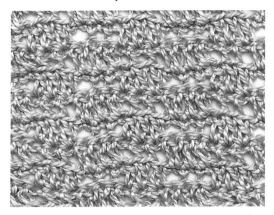

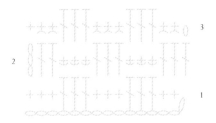

Row 1: 1 DC in 2nd ch from hook, 1 DC in next ch, *1 TR in each of next 3 ch, 1 DC in each of following 3 ch, repeat from * to end, turn.

Row 2: 3 CH, skip first dc, 1 TR in each of 2 dc, *1 DC in front loop of each of 3 tr, 1 TR in each of 3 dc, repeat from *, working last TR in 1 ch, turn.

Row 3: 1 CH, skip first tr, 1 DC in back loop of each of 2 tr, *1 TR in each of 3 dc, 1 DC in back loop of each of 3 tr, repeat from * to end, working last DC in 3rd of 3 ch, turn.

Repeat rows 2 and 3.

Wavy chevrons

A multiple of 8 sts (add 3 for foundation ch).

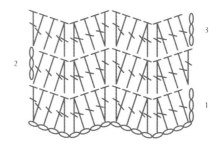

Row 1: 1 TR in 4th ch from hook, 1 TR in next ch, [2 TR TOG over next 2 ch] twice, 1 TR in next ch, 2 TR in next ch, *2 TR in next ch, 1 TR in next ch, [2 TR TOG over next 2 ch] twice, 1 TR in next ch, 2 TR in next ch, repeat from * to end, turn.

Row 2: 3 CH, 1 TR in first tr, 1 TR in next tr, [2 TR TOG over next 2 sts] twice, 1 TR in next tr, 2 TR in next tr, *2 TR in next tr, 1 TR in next tr, [2 TR TOG over next 2 sts] twice, 1 TR in next tr, 2 TR in next tr, repeat from *, working last 2 TR in 3rd of 3 ch, turn.
Repeat row 2.

Wide chevrons

A multiple of 14 sts + 1 (add 3 for foundation ch).

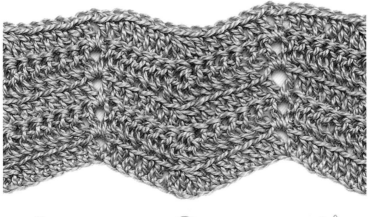

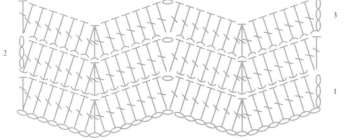

Row 1: 1 TR in 4th ch from hook, *1 TR in each of 5 ch, 3 TR TOG over next 3 ch, 1 TR in each of 5 ch, [1 TR, 1 CH, 1 TR] in next ch, repeat from *, ending 2 TR in last ch, turn.
Row 2: 3 CH, 1 TR in front loop of first tr, *1 TR in front loop of each of 5 tr, 3 TR TOG over front loops of next 3 tr, 1 TR in front loop of each of 5 tr, [1 TR, 1 CH, 1 TR] in 1 ch sp, repeat from *, ending 2 TR in 3rd of 3 ch, turn.
Row 3: As row 2, but working in back loops of sts.
Repeat rows 2 and 3.

Chain loop stitch

Any number of sts (add 2 for foundation ch) – make foundation ch
loosely. The chain loops may be made to any desired length.

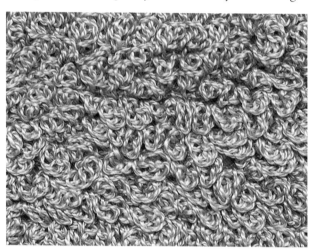

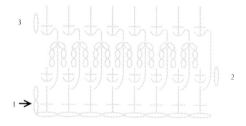

Row 1 (wrong side row): 1
EXDC in 3rd ch from hook, 1
EXDC in each ch to end, turn.
Row 2: 1 CH, 1 DC in front
loop of first exdc, *6 ch, 1 DC
in front loop of next exdc,
repeat from *, ending 1 DC in
front loop of last exdc, turn.

Row 3: 1 CH, 1 EXDC in
empty loop of first exdc 2 rows
below, 1 EXDC in empty loop of
each exdc 2 rows below to end,
turn.
Repeat rows 2 and 3.

Fans and Shells

3

Fans are formed when several long stitches (such as trebles) are worked into the same place. Sometimes the formation is flat, just like a fan, but some variations are more rounded and may be referred to as "shells".

Close scallops

A multiple of 5 sts + 3 (multiples of 6 sts + 1 for foundation ch).

Row 1: 2 TR in 4th ch from hook, skip 2 ch, 1 DC in next ch, *skip 2 ch, 4 TR in next ch, skip 2 ch, 1 DC in next ch, repeat from * to end, turn.

Row 2: 3 CH, 2 TR in first dc, skip 2 tr, *1 DC between 2nd and 3rd tr of next group, skip 2 tr, 4 TR in next dc, skip 2 tr, repeat from *, ending 1 DC in sp between last tr and 3 ch, turn.

Repeat row 2.

Open scallop stitch

A multiple of 6 sts + 1.

Special stitch – GP (group): 2 linked trebles, worked as follows: *yrh, insert hook in next st, yrh, pull loop through, yrh, pull through first 2 loops*, skip next 3 sts, repeat * to * in next st, yrh, pull through first 2 loops, yrh, pull through both loops on hook.

Row 1: [2 TR, 1 CH, 2 TR] in 4th ch from hook, *1 GP, [2 TR, 1 CH, 2 TR] in next ch, repeat from * to last 3 ch, 1 GP ending in last ch, turn.

Row 2: 3 CH, skip [first gp, 1 tr], 1 TR in next tr, *[2 TR, 1 CH, 2 TR] in 1 ch sp, 1 GP, repeat from *, ending last GP in 3rd of 3 ch, turn.

Repeat row 2.

Rope stitch

A multiple of 3 sts + 2 (add 1 for foundation ch).

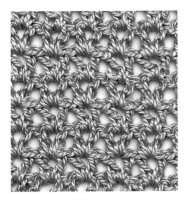

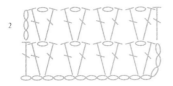

Row 1: 1 TR in 4th ch from hook, 1 CH, 1 TR in next ch, *skip 1 ch, 1 TR in next ch, 1 CH, 1 TR in next ch, repeat from * to last ch, 1 TR in last ch, turn.

Row 2: 3 CH, skip first 2 tr, *[1 TR, 1 CH, 1 TR] in 1 ch sp, skip 2 tr, repeat from *, ending skip last tr, 1 TR in 3rd of 3 ch, turn.

Repeat row 2.

Tulip stitch

A multiple of 4 sts (add 5 for foundation ch).

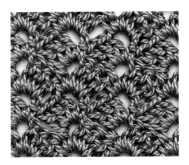

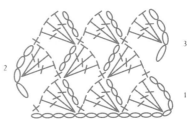

Row 1: 3 TR in 5th ch from hook, skip 3 ch, 1 DC in next ch, *3 CH, 3 TR in same ch as last dc, skip 3 ch, 1 DC in next ch, repeat from *, ending 1 DC in last ch, turn.

Row 2: 4 CH, 3 TR in first of these 4 ch, skip [1 dc, 3 tr], 1 DC in 3 ch sp, *3 CH, 3 TR in same ch sp as last dc, skip [1 dc, 3 tr], 1 DC in next 3 ch sp, repeat from *, working last DC under 4 ch, turn.

Repeat row 2.

STITCH KEY

○
chain

+
double crochet

T
treble

Special Stitches

group of 2 linked trebles

Peacock stitch

A multiple of 10 sts + 1 (add 1 for foundation ch).

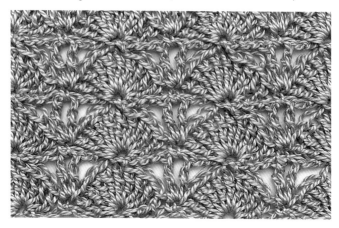

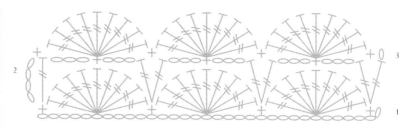

Row 1: 1 DC in 2nd ch from hook, *skip 4 ch, 9 DTR in next ch, skip 4 ch, 1 DC in next ch, repeat from * to end, turn.

Row 2: 4 CH, 1 DTR in first dc, *3 CH, skip 4 dtr, 1 DC in next dtr (the centre dtr of 9), 3 CH, skip 4 dtr, 2 DTR in next dc, repeat from *, ending 2 DTR in last dc, turn.

Row 3: 1 CH, 1 DC in sp between first 2 dtr, *skip 3 ch, 9 DTR in next dc, skip 3 ch, 1 DC in sp between 2 dtr, repeat from *, ending 1 DC in sp between last dtr and turning ch, turn.

Repeat rows 2 and 3.

Clam stitch

A multiple of 10 sts + 2 (add 2 for foundation ch).

Row 3: 3 CH, skip first tr, *[1 TR in 2 tr tog, 1 TR in 1 ch sp] twice, 1 TR in 2 tr tog, 1 TR in each of 5 tr, repeat from *, ending 1 TR in 3rd of 3 ch, turn.

Row 4: 3 CH, skip first tr, *skip next 2 tr, [2 TR TOG, 1 CH] twice in next tr, 2 TR TOG in same tr, skip 2 tr, 1 TR in each of next 5 tr, repeat from *, ending 1 TR in 3rd of 3 ch, turn.

Row 5: 3 CH, skip first tr, *1 TR in each of next 5 tr, [1 TR in 2 tr tog, 1 TR in 1 ch sp] twice, 1 TR in 2 tr tog, repeat from *, ending 1 TR in 3rd of 3 ch, turn.

Repeat rows 2–5.

Row 1: 1 TR in 4th ch from hook, 1 TR in each ch to end, turn.

Row 2: 3 CH, skip first tr, *1 TR in each of next 5 tr, skip 2 tr, [2 TR TOG, 1 CH] twice in next tr, 2 TR TOG in same tr, skip 2 tr, repeat from *, ending 1 TR in 3rd of 3 ch, turn.

STITCH KEY

o
chain

+
double crochet

treble

double treble

2 trebles together in same place

Paris stitch

A multiple of 3 sts (add 1 for foundation ch).

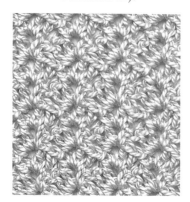

2

1

Row 1: 1 TR in 4th ch from hook, 2 CH, 1 DC in same ch as last tr, *skip 2 ch, [2 TR, 2 CH, 1 DC] in next ch, repeat from * to end, turn.
Row 2: 3 CH, skip first dc, [1 TR, 2 CH, 1 DC] in first 2 ch sp, *skip [2 tr and 1 dc], [2 TR, 2 CH, 1 DC] in next 2 ch sp, repeat from * to end, turn.
Repeat row 2.

Iris stitch

A multiple of 4 sts + 1 (add 2 for foundation ch).

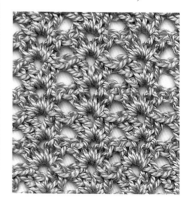

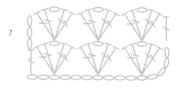

2

1

Row 1: [2 TR, 1 CH, 2 TR] in 5th ch from hook, *skip 3 ch, [2 TR, 1 CH, 2 TR] in next ch, repeat from * to last 2 ch, skip 1 ch, 1 TR in last ch, turn.
Row 2: 3 CH, skip first 3 tr *[2 TR, 1 CH, 2 TR] in 1 ch sp, skip next 4 tr, repeat from *, ending skip last 2 tr, 1 TR in next ch, turn.
Repeat row 2.

Arcade stitch

A multiple of 6 sts + 1.

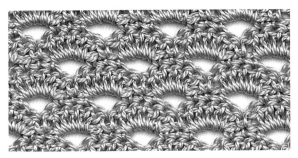

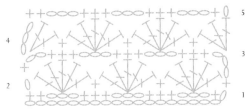

Row 1: 1 DC in 2nd ch from hook, *3 CH, skip 3 ch, 1 DC in each of next 3 ch, repeat from *, ending 1 DC in each of last 2 ch, turn.

Row 2: 1 CH, skip first dc, *skip 1 dc, 5 TR in 3 ch sp, skip 1 dc, 1 DC in next dc (the centre dc of 3), repeat from *, ending 1 DC in 1 ch, turn.

Row 3: 3 CH, skip [1 dc, 1 tr], *1 DC in each of next 3 tr (the centre 3 tr of 5), 3 CH, skip [1 tr, 1 dc, 1 tr], repeat from * to last group, 1 DC in each of 3 tr, 2 ch, skip 1 tr, 1 DC in 1 ch, turn.

Row 4: 3 CH, skip first dc, 2 TR in 2 ch sp, *skip 1 dc, 1 DC in next dc (the centre dc of 3), skip 1 dc, 5 TR in 3 ch sp, repeat from *, ending 3 TR under 3 ch, turn.

Row 5: 1 CH, skip first tr, 1 DC in next tr, *3 CH, skip [1 tr, 1 dc, 1 tr], 1 DC in each of next 3 tr (the centre 3 tr of 5), repeat from *, ending 1 DC in last tr, 1 DC in 3rd of 3 ch, turn.

Repeat rows 2–5.

STITCH KEY

o
chain

+
double crochet

T
treble

Blossom stitch

A multiple of 4 sts + 1.

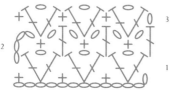

Row 1: [1 TR, 1 CH, 1 TR] in 3rd ch from hook, *skip 1 ch, 1 DC in next ch, skip 1 ch, [1 TR, 1 CH, 1 TR] in next ch, repeat from * to last 2 ch, skip 1 ch, 1 DC in last ch, turn.
Row 2: 4 CH, skip [first dc, 1 tr], *1 DC in 1 ch sp, 1 CH, skip 1 tr, 1 TR in dc, 1 CH, skip 1 tr, repeat from *, ending 1 DC in last ch sp, 1 CH, skip 1 tr, 1 TR in next ch, turn.
Row 3: 1 CH, skip first tr, *skip 1 ch, [1 TR, 1 CH, 1 TR] in dc, skip 1 ch, 1 DC in tr, repeat from *, working last DC in 3rd of 4 ch, turn.
Repeat rows 2 and 3.

Turtle stitch

A multiple of 6 sts + 4 (add 3 for foundation ch).

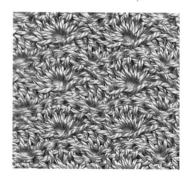

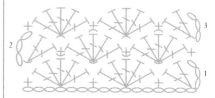

Row 1: 2 TR in 4th ch from hook, skip 2 ch, *1 DC in next ch, skip 2 ch, 5 TR in next ch, skip 2 ch, repeat from *, ending 1 DC in last ch, turn.
Row 2: 3 CH, 2 TR in front loop of first dc, skip 2 tr, *1 DC in front loop of next tr (the centre tr of 5), skip 2 tr, 5 TR in front loop of next dc, skip 2 tr, repeat from *, ending 1 DC in 3rd of 3 ch, turn.
Row 3: As row 2, but working in back loops of sts.
Repeat rows 2 and 3.

Large shell stitch

A multiple of 8 sts + 5 (add 4 for foundation ch).

Row 1: 3 DTR in 5th ch from hook, * skip 3 ch, 1 DC in next ch, skip 3 ch, 7 DTR in next ch, repeat from * to last 4 ch, skip 3 ch, 1 DC in last ch, turn.
Row 2: 4 CH, 3 DTR in first dc, * skip 3 dtr, 1 DC in next dtr (the centre dtr of 7), skip 3 dtr, 7 DTR in next dc, repeat from * ending 1 DC in 4th of 4 ch, turn.
Repeat row 2.

Sprig stitch

A multiple of 4 sts + 2 (add 1 for foundation ch).

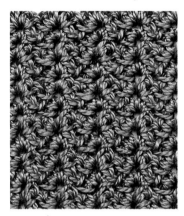

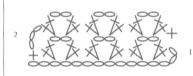

Row 1: 2 DC in 4th ch from hook, 2 CH, 2 DC in next ch, *skip 2 ch, 2 DC in next ch, 2 CH, 2 DC in next ch, repeat from * to last 2 ch, skip 1 ch, 1 DC in last ch, turn.
Row 2: 3 CH, [2 DC, 2 CH, 2 DC] in each 2 ch sp, ending 1 DC in 3rd of 3 ch, turn.
Repeat row 2.

STITCH KEY

○
chain

+
double crochet

treble

double treble

double crochet in front loop only

double crochet in back loop only

treble in front loop only

treble in back loop only

2 double crochet in same place

Thistle stitch

A multiple of 7 sts + 2 (add 2 for foundation ch).

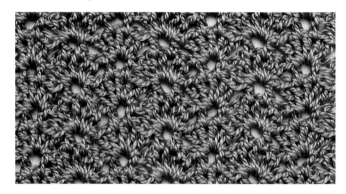

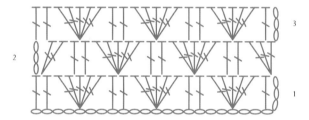

Row 1: 1 TR in 4th ch from hook, *skip 2 ch, 5 TR in next ch, skip 2 ch, 1 TR in each of next 2 ch, repeat from * to end, turn.

Row 2: 3 CH, 2 TR in first tr, skip 3 tr, *1 TR in sp between 2nd and 3rd tr of group, 1 TR in sp between 3rd and 4th tr of group, skip 3 tr, 5 TR in sp between 2 vertical tr, skip 3 tr, repeat from *, ending 3 TR in sp between last tr and 3 ch, turn.

Row 3: 3 CH, 1 TR between first 2 tr, *skip 3 tr, 5 TR in sp between 2 vertical tr, skip 3 tr, 1 TR in sp between 2nd and 3rd tr of group, 1 TR in sp between 3rd and 4th tr of group, repeat from *, ending 1 TR in sp between last tr and 3 ch, 1 TR in 3rd of 3 ch, turn.

Repeat rows 2 and 3.

Parquet stitch

A multiple of 3 sts + 1 (add 2 for foundation ch).

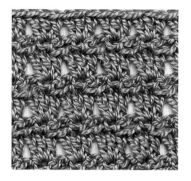

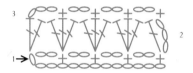

Row 1 (wrong side row): 1 DC in 6th ch from hook, *2 CH, skip 2 ch, 1 DC in next ch, repeat from * to end, turn.
Row 2: 3 CH, 1 TR in first dc, *skip 2 ch, 3 TR in next dc, repeat from *, ending skip 2 ch, 2 TR in next ch, turn.
Row 3: 1 CH, skip first tr, *2 CH, skip 2 tr, 1 DC in next tr (the centre tr of 3), repeat from *, ending 1 DC in 3rd of 3 ch, turn.
Repeat rows 2 and 3.

Ripple stitch

A multiple of 3 sts + 1 (add 2 for foundation ch).

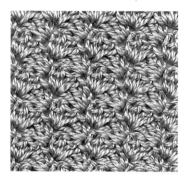

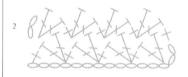

Row 1: 2 TR in 3rd ch from hook, *skip 2 ch, [1 DC, 2 TR] in next ch, repeat from * to last 3 ch, skip 2 ch, 1 DC in last ch, turn.
Row 2: 2 CH, 2 TR in first dc, *skip 2 tr, [1 DC, 2 TR] in next dc, repeat from *, ending skip 2 tr, 1 DC in 2nd of 2 ch, turn.
Repeat row 2.

STITCH KEY

○
chain

+
double crochet

⊤
treble

Little fans

A multiple of 6 sts + 1 (add 1 for foundation ch).

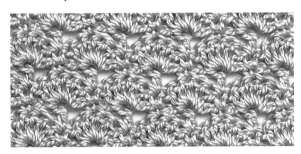

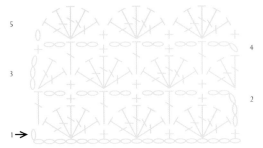

Row 1 (wrong side row): 5 TR in 5th ch from hook, skip 2 ch, 1 DC in next ch, *skip 2 ch, 5 TR in next ch, skip 2 ch, 1 DC in next ch, repeat from * to end, turn.

Row 2: 5 CH, skip [first dc, 2 tr], *1 DC in next tr (the centre tr of 5), 2 CH, skip 2 tr, 1 TR in dc, 2 CH, skip 2 tr, repeat from *, ending 1 TR in next ch, turn.

Row 3: 3 CH, 2 TR in first tr, *skip 2 ch, 1 DC in dc, skip 2 ch, 5 TR in tr, repeat from *, ending 3 TR in 3rd of 5 ch, turn.

Row 4: 1 CH, skip first tr, *2 CH, skip 2 tr, 1 TR in dc, 2 CH, skip 2 tr, 1 DC in next tr (the centre tr of 5), repeat from *, ending 1 DC in 3rd of 3 ch, turn.

Row 5: 1 CH, skip first dc, *skip 2 ch, 5 TR in tr, skip 2 ch, 1 DC in dc, repeat from *, working last DC in first of 3 ch, turn.

Repeat rows 2–5.

Starburst stitch

A multiple of 10 sts + 1 (for foundation ch, multiples of 8 sts + 1).

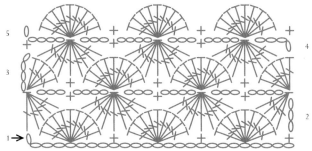

Row 1 (wrong side row):
Skip 4 ch, *9 TR in next ch, skip 3 ch, 1 DC in next ch, skip 3 ch, repeat from *, ending 1 DC in last ch, turn.

Row 2: 3 CH, skip first dc, 4 TR TOG over next 4 tr, *4 CH, 1 DC in next tr (the centre tr of 9), 3 CH, 9 TR TOG over [next 4 tr, 1 dc, 4 tr], repeat from *, ending 5 TR TOG over [last 4 tr and 1 ch].

Row 3: 4 CH, 4 TR in top of 5 tr tog, *skip 3 ch, 1 DC in dc, skip 4 ch, 9 TR in top of 9 tr tog, repeat from *, ending 5 TR in top of 4 tr tog, turn.

Row 4: 4 CH, skip first tr, *9 TR TOG over [next 4 tr, 1 dc, 4 tr], 4 CH, 1 DC in next tr (the centre tr of 9), 3 CH, repeat from *, ending 1 DC in 4th of 4 ch, turn.

Row 5: 1 CH, skip first dc, *skip 4 ch, 9 TR in top of 9 tr tog, skip 3 ch, 1 DC in dc, repeat from *, working last DC in first of 4 ch, turn.

Repeat rows 2–5.

STITCH KEY

◯ chain

+ double crochet

⊥ treble

✹ 9 trebles together

→ direction of work

4 *Mesh and Filet Stitches*

Simple mesh patterns may be used alone, as the basis for other stitches, or as a background for appliqué motifs. Mesh patterns may also be embellished by weaving or by surface crochet. Other mesh patterns, such as Solomon's grid and crazy picot mesh, are more decorative in themselves.

Small mesh ground

Odd number of sts (add 3 for foundation ch).

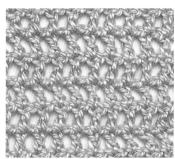

Row 1: 1 TR in 6th ch from hook, *1 CH, skip 1 ch, 1 TR in next ch, repeat from * to end, turn.
Row 2: 4 CH, skip [first tr, 1 ch], *1 TR in next tr, 1 CH, skip 1 ch, repeat from *, ending 1 TR in next ch, turn.
Repeat row 2.

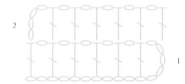

Large mesh ground

A multiple of 3 sts + 1, (add 4 for foundation ch).

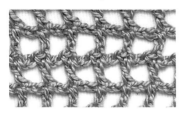

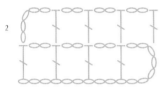

Row 1: 1 TR in 8th ch from hook, *2 CH, skip 2 ch, 1 TR in next ch, repeat from * to end, turn.

Row 2: 5 CH, skip first tr and 2 ch, *1 TR in next tr, 2 CH, skip 2 ch, repeat from *, ending 1 TR in next ch, turn.

Repeat row 2.

Arch mesh

A multiple of 4 sts + 1 (add 5 for foundation ch).

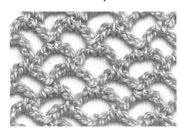

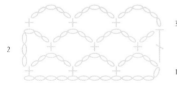

Row 1: 1 DC in 10th ch from hook, *5 CH, skip 3 ch, 1 DC in next ch, repeat from * to end, turn.

Row 2: 6 CH, *1 DC in next ch sp, 5 CH, repeat from *, ending 1 DC in last ch sp, 2 CH, 1 TR in 4th of 9 ch, turn.

Row 3: 6 CH, 1 DC in first 5 ch sp, *5 CH, 1 DC in next ch sp, repeat from * to end, turn.

Row 4: As row 2, ending 1 TR in first of 6 ch, turn.

Repeat rows 3 and 4.

TIP

For a firmer fabric, work the double crochet in the centre chain of 5, instead of in the chain space.

STITCH KEY

○ chain

+ double crochet

⊤ treble

Filet squares

A multiple of 12 sts + 1 (add 2 for foundation ch).

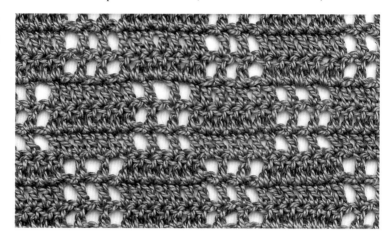

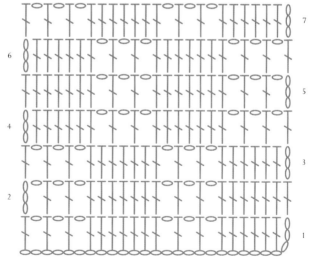

Row 1: 1 TR in 4th ch from hook, 1 TR in each of next 5 ch, [1 CH, skip 1 ch, 1 TR in next ch] 3 times, *1 TR in each of next 6 ch, [1 CH, skip 1 ch, 1 TR in next ch] 3 times, repeat

from * to end, turn.

Row 2: 4 CH, skip [first tr, 1 ch], 1 TR in next tr, [1 CH, skip 1 ch, 1 TR in next tr] twice, 1 TR in each of next 6 tr, *[1 CH, skip 1 ch, 1 TR in next tr] 3 times, 1 TR in each of next 6 tr, repeat from * ending 1 TR in 3rd of 3 ch, turn.

Row 3: 3 CH, skip first tr, *1 TR in each of next 6 tr, [1 CH, skip 1 ch, 1 TR in next tr] 3 times, repeat from *, working last TR in 3rd of 4 ch, turn.

Row 4: 3 CH, skip first tr, *[1 TR in 1 ch sp, 1 TR in tr] 3 times, [1 CH, skip 1 tr, 1 TR in next tr] 3 times, repeat from *, working last TR in 3rd of 3 ch, turn.

Row 5: As row 2.
Row 6: As row 3.
Row 7: As row 4.
Repeat rows 2–7.

Picot arch mesh

A multiple of 5 sts + 3 (for foundation ch, multiples of 4 ch + 4).

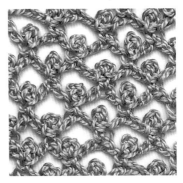

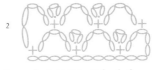

Row 1: 1 DC in 8th ch from hook, 3 CH, 1 SS in dc just made, *5 CH, skip 3 ch, 1 DC in next ch, 3 CH, 1 SS in dc just made, repeat from *, ending 1 DC in last ch, turn.

Row 2: 5 CH, skip first dc, *1 DC in 3rd of 5 ch, 3 CH, 1 SS in dc just made, 5 CH, skip [next dc, picot], repeat from *, ending 1 DC in 3rd of 7 ch, turn.

Repeat row 2, ending 1 DC in 3rd of 5 ch.

STITCH KEY

○ chain

• slip stitch

+ double crochet

⊤ treble

🜀 3 chain picot

Honeycomb

A multiple of 4 sts + 3 (add 5 for foundation ch).

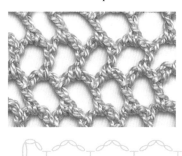

Row 1: 1 TR in 8th ch from hook, *4 CH, skip 3 ch, 1 TR in next ch, repeat from * to end, turn.
Row 2: 5 CH, 1 TR in first ch sp, *4 CH, 1 TR in next ch sp, repeat from * to end, turn. Repeat row 2.

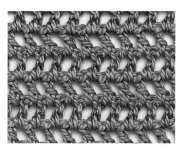

Offset filet net

Even number of sts (add 3 for foundation ch).

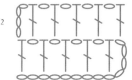

Row 1: 1 TR in 5th ch from hook, *1 CH, skip 1 ch, 1 TR in next ch, repeat from * to end, turn.
Row 2: 4 CH, skip first tr, *1 TR in next ch sp, 1 CH, skip 1 tr, repeat from *, ending 1 TR under 4 ch, turn. Repeat row 2.

Solomon's knot

A multiple of 3 sts + 1 (for foundation ch, multiples of 4 ch + 2).

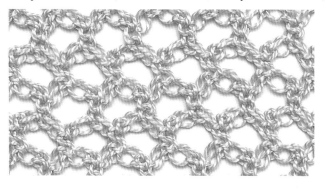

Special stitch – SK (Solomon's knot): Draw up loop on hook to about ½ in. (12mm), 1 CH, insert hook under left-hand thread of 3 threads below hook, work 1 DC to close the knot (see page 38).

Row 1: 1 DC in 2nd ch from hook, *2 SK, skip 3 ch, 1 DC in next ch, repeat from * to end, turn.

Row 2: 5 CH, 1 SK, skip [first dc, 1 sk], *1 DC in closing dc of next sk, 2 SK, skip [loop of same sk, 1 dc, 1 sk], repeat from *, ending 1 DC in closing dc of last sk, 1 SK, 1 TRTR in dc, turn.

Row 3: 1 CH, 1 DC in closing dc of first sk, *2 SK, skip [loop of same sk, 1 dc, 1sk], 1 DC in closing dc of next sk, repeat from *, working last DC in 5th of 5 ch, turn.

Repeat rows 2 and 3.

Solomon's grid

Odd number of sts (for foundation ch, multiples of 4 ch + 3).

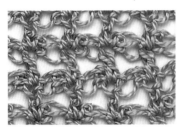

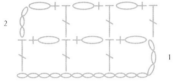

Special stitch – SK (Solomon's knot, see page 91)

Row 1: 1 SK, skip 6 ch, 1 TR in next ch, *1 SK, skip 3 ch, 1 TR in next ch, repeat from * to end, turn.

Row 2: 3 CH, skip first tr, *1 SK, skip 1 sk, 1 TR in tr, repeat from *, ending 1 TR in 6th of 6 ch, turn.

Repeat row 2, ending 1 TR in 3rd of 3 ch.

Triangle mesh

A multiple of 6 sts + 1 (add 6 for foundation ch).

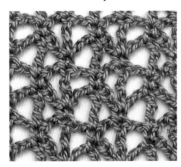

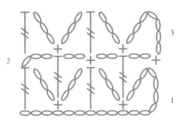

Row 1: 1 DC in 10th ch from hook, *3 CH, skip 2 ch, 1 DTR in next ch, 3 CH, skip 2 ch, 1 DC in next ch, repeat from * ending 1 DTR in last ch, turn.

Row 2: 1 CH, skip first dtr, *2 CH, skip 3 ch, 1 DTR in dc, 2 CH, skip 3 ch, 1 DC in dtr, repeat from *, ending skip 3 ch, 1 DC in next ch, turn.

Row 3: 7 CH, skip [1 dc, 2 ch], *1 DC in dtr, 3 CH, skip 2 ch, 1 DTR in dc, 3 CH, skip 2 ch, repeat from *, ending 1 DTR in last ch, turn.

Repeat rows 2 and 3.

Ladder stitch

A multiple of 6 sts + 1 (add 6 for foundation ch).

Row 1: [1 DC, 3 CH, 1 DC] in 13th ch from hook, *5 CH, skip 5 ch, [1 DC, 3 CH, 1 DC] in next ch, repeat from *, ending 5 CH, skip 5 ch, 1 EXDC in last ch, turn.

Row 2: 7 CH, skip first exdc, * skip 5 ch, [1 DC, 3 CH, 1 DC] in next 3 ch loop, 5 CH, repeat from *, ending 5 CH, skip 5 ch, 1 EXDC in next ch, turn.

Repeat row 2.

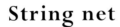

String net

A multiple of 4 sts + 1 (add 5 for foundation ch).

Row 1: 1 TR in 10th ch from hook, *3 CH, skip 3 ch, 1 TR in next ch, repeat from * to end, turn.

Row 2: 1 CH, skip first tr, *3 CH, skip 3 ch, 1 DC in next tr, repeat from *, ending skip 3 ch, 1 DC in next ch, turn.

Row 3: 6 CH, skip [1 dc, 3 ch], *1 TR in next dc, 3 CH, skip 3 ch, repeat from *, ending 1 TR in last ch, turn.

Repeat rows 2 and 3.

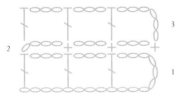

STITCH KEY

○
chain

+
double crochet

┴
extended double crochet

treble

double treble

Special Stitches

Solomon's knot

4

Bar and lattice stitch

A multiple of 4 sts + 1 (add 5 for foundation ch).

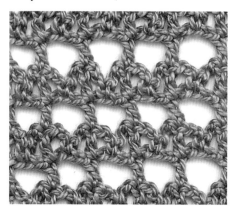

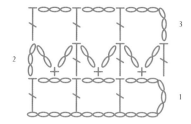

Row 1: 1 TR in 10th ch from hook, *3 CH, skip 3 ch, 1 TR in next ch, repeat from * to end, turn.

Row 2: 5 CH, skip [first tr and 1 ch], 1 DC in next ch, 2 CH, skip 1 ch, *1 TR in tr, 2 CH, skip 1 ch, 1 DC in next ch, 2 CH, skip 1 ch, repeat from *, ending 1 TR in next ch, turn.

Row 3: 6 CH, skip [first tr, 2 ch, 1 dc, 2 ch], *1 TR in next tr, 3 CH, skip [2 ch, 1 dc, 2 ch], repeat from *, ending 1 TR in next ch, turn.

Repeat rows 2 and 3.

Open checker stitch

A multiple of 6 sts (add 3 for foundation ch).

Row 1: 1 TR in 4th ch from hook, 1 TR in next ch, *3 CH, skip 3 ch, 1 TR in each of next 3 ch, repeat from *, ending 3 CH, skip 3 ch, 1 TR in last ch, turn.
Row 2: 3 CH, skip first tr, 2 TR in first 3 ch sp, *3 CH, skip 3 tr, 3 TR in next 3 ch sp, repeat from *, ending 3 CH, skip 2 tr, 1 TR in 3rd of 3 ch, turn.
Repeat row 2.

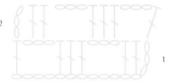

Firm mesh

A multiple of 4 sts + 1 (add 1 for foundation ch).

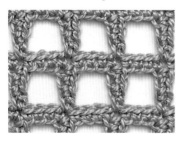

Row 2: 9 CH, skip first 4 dc, 1 SS in next dc, turn, 1 DC in each of first 3 ch, *6 CH, skip next 3 dc of previous row, 1 SS in next dc, turn, 1 DC in each of first 3 ch, repeat from * to end, turn.
Row 3: 1 CH, 1 DC in same ch as last dc of previous row, *1 DC in each of next 3 ch, 1 DC in same ch as top dc of stem, repeat from *, working last DC in 3rd of 3 empty ch at beginning of previous row, turn. Repeat rows 2 and 3.

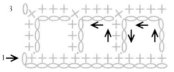

Row 1 (wrong side row): 1 DC in 2nd ch from hook, 1 DC in each ch to end, turn.

STITCH KEY

o
chain

·
slip stitch

+
double crochet

T
treble

➜
direction of work

Picot lattice

A multiple of 4 sts + 1 (add 5 for foundation ch).

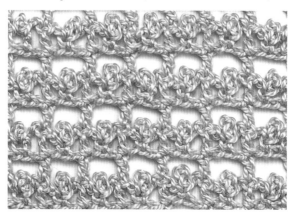

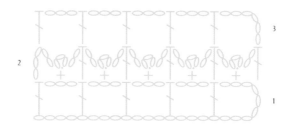

Row 1: 1 TR in 10th ch from hook, *3 CH, skip 3 ch, 1 TR in next ch, repeat from * to end, turn.

Row 2: 5 CH, skip [first tr, 1 ch], 1 DC in next ch, 3 CH, 1 SS in dc just made, 2 CH, skip 1 ch, *1 TR in tr, 2 CH, skip 1 ch, 1 DC in next ch, 3 CH, 1 SS in dc just made, 2 CH, skip 1 ch, repeat from *, ending 1 TR in next ch, turn.

Row 3: 6 CH, skip [first tr, 2 ch, picot, 2 ch], *1 TR in tr, 3 CH, skip [2 ch, picot, 2 ch], repeat from *, ending 1 TR in next ch, turn.

Repeat rows 2 and 3.

Crazy picot mesh

A multiple of 7 sts (for foundation ch, multiples of 5 ch + 8).

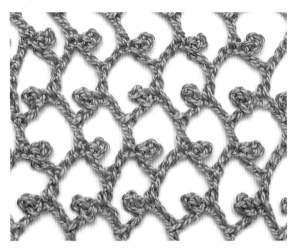

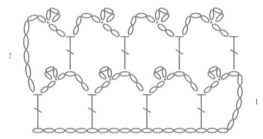

Row 1: 1 SS in 4th ch from hook, 2 CH, skip 8 ch, 1 TR in next ch, *7 CH, 1 SS in 4th ch from hook, 2 CH, skip 4 foundation ch, 1 TR in next ch, repeat from * to end, turn.
Row 2: 10 CH, 1 SS in 4th ch from hook, 2 CH, skip [first tr, 2 ch, 1 picot], 1 TR in 3rd ch before tr, *7 CH, 1 SS in 4th ch from hook, 2 CH, skip [2 ch, 1 tr, 2 ch, 1 picot], 1 TR in 3rd ch before tr, repeat from * to end, turn.
Repeat row 2.

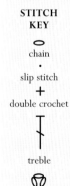

STITCH KEY

○ chain

· slip stitch

+ double crochet

🙼 treble

♀ 3 chain picot

5 Openwork and Lace Stitches

Several different techniques may be used to create openwork and lacy patterns. Open areas formed by working a chain and skipping stitches are contrasted with solid areas formed by working several stitches in the same place. Picots may be added to decorate a space, and stitches of different lengths can be used along a row to create wavy effects.

Lacy scallops

A multiple of 7 sts + 2 (multiple of 6 ch + 4 for foundation ch).

Row 1: [2 TR, 3 CH, 2 TR] in 6th ch from hook, *skip 5 ch, [2 TR, 3 CH, 2 TR] in next ch, repeat from * to last 4 ch, skip 3 ch, 1 TR in last ch, turn.

Row 2: 3 CH, skip first 3 tr, *[2 TR, 3 CH, 2 TR] in 3 ch sp, skip next 4 tr, repeat from *, ending skip last 2 tr, 1 TR in 5th of 5 ch, turn.

Repeat row 2, ending 1 TR in 3rd of 3 ch, turn.

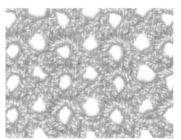

Offset scallops

A multiple of 4 sts (add 2 for foundation ch).

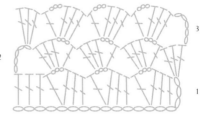

Row 1: 1 TR in 4th ch from hook, 1 TR in next ch, *[1 TR, 3 CH, 1 TR] in next ch, skip 1 ch, 1 TR in each of next 2 ch, repeat from * to last ch, 1 TR in last ch, turn.
Row 2: 5 CH, skip first 4 tr, * [3 TR, 3 CH, 1 TR] in 3 ch sp, skip next 4 tr, repeat from *, ending skip last 3 tr, 3 TR in 3rd of 3 ch, turn.
Repeat row 2, ending 3 TR in 5th of 5 ch, turn.

Lozenge stitch

A multiple of 6 sts + 4 (add 4 for foundation ch).

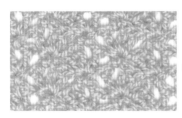

Row 1: 2 TR in 5th ch from hook, 1 CH, skip 2 ch, 1 DC in next ch, *1 CH, skip 2 ch, [1 TR, 2 CH, 2 TR] in next ch, 1 CH, skip 2 ch, 1 DC in next ch, repeat from * to end, turn.
Row 2: 4 CH, 2 TR in first dc, 1 CH, skip [1 ch, 2 tr], *1 DC in 2 ch sp, 1 CH, skip [1 tr, 1 ch], [1 TR, 1 CH, 2 TR] in next dc, 1 CH, skip [1 ch, 2 tr], repeat from *, ending 1 DC under 4 ch, turn.
Repeat row 2.

STITCH KEY

o
chain

+
double crochet

T
treble

5

OPENWORK AND LACE STITCHES

Fan trellis stitch

A multiple of 12 sts + 1, (add 6 for foundation ch).

Row 1 (wrong side row): 1 DC in 11th ch from hook, *5 CH, skip 3 ch, 1 DC in next ch, repeat from * to end, turn.

Row 2: 5 CH, skip first dc, 1 DC in 5 ch sp, *skip 1 dc, 7 TR in next 5 ch sp, skip 1 dc, 1 DC in next 5 ch sp, 5 CH, skip 1 dc, 1 DC in next 5 ch sp, repeat from *, ending 1 DC in last ch sp, 2 CH, 1 TR in 6th ch from last dc of previous row, turn.

Row 3: 6 CH, skip [1 tr, 2 ch, 1 dc, 1 tr], *1 DC in next tr (the 2nd of 7), 5 CH, skip 3 tr, 1 DC in next tr (the 6th of 7), 5 CH, skip [1 tr, 1 dc], 1 DC in 5 ch sp, 5 CH, skip [1 dc, 1 tr], repeat from *, ending 1 DC under 5 ch, turn.

Repeat rows 2 and 3.

100

Sultan stitch

A multiple of 4 sts + 2 (add 3 for foundation ch).

Row 1: [1 TR, 2 CH, 1 TR] in 6th ch from hook, *skip 3 ch, [1 TR, 2 CH, 1 TR] in next ch, repeat from * to last 3 ch, skip 2 ch, 1 TR in last ch, turn.

Row 2: 3 CH, skip first 2 tr, *4 TR in 2 ch sp, skip 2 tr, repeat from *, ending skip last tr, 1 TR in next ch, turn.

Row 3: 4 CH, 1 TR in sp between first 2 tr, *skip group of 4 tr, [1 TR, 2 CH, 1 TR] in sp before next group, repeat from *, ending [1 TR, 1 CH, 1 TR] in sp before 3 ch, turn.

Row 4: 3 CH, skip first tr, 2 TR in 1 ch sp, *skip 2 tr, 4 TR in 2 ch sp, repeat from *, ending 3 TR under 4 ch, turn.

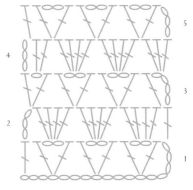

Row 5: 3 CH, skip first 3 tr, * [1 TR, 2 CH, 1 TR] in sp before next group, skip group of 4 tr, repeat from *, ending skip last 2 tr, 1 TR in sp before 3 ch, turn. Repeat rows 2–5.

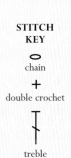

Star stitch

A multiple of 4 sts + 2 (add 3 for foundation ch).

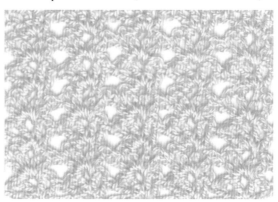

Row 1: [1 TR, 1 CH] 3 times all in 6th ch from hook, 1 TR in same ch, *skip 3 ch, [1 TR, 1 CH] 3 times in next ch, 1 TR in same ch, repeat from * to last 3 ch, skip 2 ch, 1 TR in last ch, turn.

Row 2: 3 CH, skip [first 2 tr, 1 ch, 1 tr], * [1 TR, 1 CH] 3 times in next ch sp, 1 TR in same ch sp, skip [1 tr, 1 ch, 2 tr, 1 ch, 1 tr], repeat from *, ending in centre of last group, skip [1 tr, 1 ch, 1 tr], 1 TR in 5th of 5 ch, turn.

Repeat row 2, ending 1 TR in 3rd of 3 ch, turn.

Spaced arches

A multiple of 8 sts + 1 (add 6 for foundation ch).

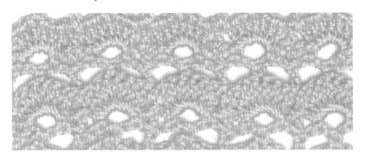

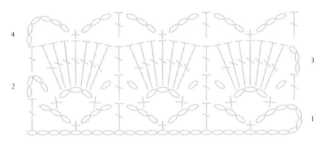

Row 1: 1 DC in 11th ch from hook, 3 CH, skip 3 ch, 1 TR in next ch, *3 CH, skip 3 ch, 1 DC in next ch, 3 CH, skip 3 ch, 1 TR in next ch, repeat from * to end, turn.

Row 2: 4 CH, skip first tr, *skip 1 ch, 1 DC in next ch, 3 CH, skip [1 ch, 1 dc, 1 ch], 1 DC in next ch, 1 CH, skip 1 ch, 1 TR in tr, 1 CH, repeat from *, working last TR in 4th ch from last dc of previous row, turn.

Row 3: 3 CH, skip first tr, *skip [1 ch, 1 dc], 7 TR in 3 ch sp, skip [1 dc, 1 ch], 1 TR in tr, repeat from *, working last TR in 2nd of 4 ch, turn.

Row 4: 6 CH, skip first 4 tr, 1 DC in next tr (the 4th of 7), 3 CH, skip 3 tr, 1 TR in next tr, *3 CH, skip 3 tr, 1 DC in next tr (the 4th of 7), 3 CH, skip 3 tr, 1 TR in next tr, repeat from *, working last TR in 3rd of 3 ch, turn.

Repeat rows 2–4.

Bridge stitch

A multiple of 8 sts + 1 (add 1 for foundation ch).

Row 1: 1 DC in 3rd ch from hook, 1 DC in next ch, *5 CH, skip 3 ch, 1 DC in each of next 5 ch, repeat from *, ending 1 DC in each of last 3 ch, turn.

Row 2: 2 CH, skip first 2 dc, *1 DC in next dc, 9 DTR in 5 ch sp, 1 DC in next dc, 2 CH, skip 3 dc, repeat from *, ending 1 CH, skip 1 dc, 1 DC in 1 ch, turn.

Row 3: 8 CH, skip [first dc, 1 ch, 1 dc, 3 dtr], *1 DC in each of next 3 dtr (the centre 3 of 9), 3 CH, skip [3 dtr, 1 dc], 1 TRTR in 2 ch sp, 3 CH, skip [1 dc, 3 dtr], repeat from *, ending 1 TRTR under 2 ch, turn.

Row 4: 4 CH, skip first trtr, *1 DC in 3 ch sp, 1 DC in each of 3 dc, 1 DC in 3 ch sp, 5 CH, skip 1 trtr, repeat from *, ending 1 DC in each of last 3 dc, 1 DC under 8 ch, 3 CH, 1 DC in 5th of 8 ch, turn.

Row 5: 4 CH, skip first dc, 4 DTR in 3 ch sp, *1 DC in next dc, 2 CH, skip 3 dc, 1 DC in next dc, 9 DTR in 5 ch sp, repeat from *, ending 5 DTR under 4 ch, turn.

Row 6: 1 CH, skip first dtr, 1 DC in next dtr, *3 CH, skip [3 dtr, 1 dc], 1 TRTR in 2 ch sp, 3 CH, skip [1 dc, 3 dtr], 1 DC in each of next 3 dtr, repeat from *, ending 1 DC in last dtr, 1 DC in 4th of 4 ch, turn.

Row 7: 1 CH, skip first dc, 1 DC in next dc, *1 DC in 3 ch sp, 5 CH, skip 1 trtr, 1 DC in next 3 ch sp, 1 DC in each of 3 dc, repeat from *, ending 1 DC in last dc, 1 DC in 1 ch, turn.

Loopy stitch

A multiple of 4 sts + 1 (add 2 for foundation ch).

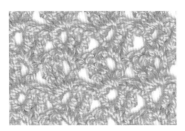

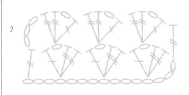

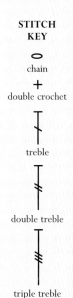

Row 1: [2 DTR, 1 CH, 1 TR] in 4th ch from hook, *skip 3 ch, [2 DTR, 1 CH, 1 TR] in next ch, repeat from * to last 3 ch, skip 2 ch, 1 DTR in last ch, turn.

Row 2: 3 CH, skip [first dtr, 1 tr], * [2 DTR, 1 CH, 1 TR] in 1 ch sp, skip [2 dtr, 1 tr], repeat from *, ending skip 2 dtr, 1 DTR in 3rd of 3 ch, turn.

Repeat row 2.

STITCH KEY

o
chain

+
double crochet

treble

double treble

triple treble

Spaced scale stitch

A multiple of 10 sts + 1 (add 3 for foundation ch).

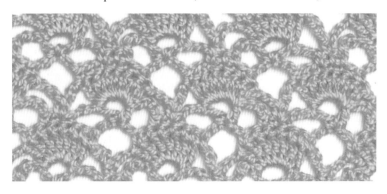

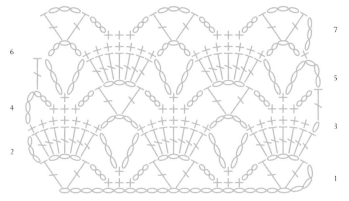

Row 1: [1 TR, 3 CH, 1 TR] in 4th ch from hook, *3 CH, skip 3 ch, 1 DC in each of next 3 ch, 3 CH, skip 3 ch, [1 TR, 3 CH, 1 TR] in next ch, repeat from * to end, turn.

Row 2: 3 CH, skip first tr, *7 TR in 3 ch sp, 3 CH, skip [1 tr, 3 ch, 1 dc], 1 DC in next dc, 3 CH, skip [1 dc, 3 ch, 1 tr], repeat from *, ending 7 TR in last 3 ch sp, turn.

Row 3: 1 CH, skip first tr, 1 DC in each of next 6 tr, *5 CH, skip [3 ch, 1 dc, 3 ch], 1 DC in each of next 7 tr, repeat from * to end, turn.

Row 4: 6 CH, skip first 2 dc, 1

DC in each of next 3 dc (the centre 3 dc of 7), *3 CH, skip [2 dc, 2 ch], [1 TR, 3 CH, 1 TR] in next ch, 3 CH, skip [2 ch, 2 dc], 1 DC in each of next 3 dc, repeat from *, ending 3 CH, skip 1 dc, 1 TR in 1 ch, turn.

Row 5: 6 CH, skip [first tr, 3 ch, 1 dc], *1 DC in next dc, 3 CH, skip [1 dc, 3 ch, 1 tr], 7 TR in next 3 ch sp, 3 CH, skip [1 tr, 3 ch, 1 dc], repeat from *, ending 3 CH, 1 TR in 3rd of 6 ch, turn.

Row 6: 5 CH, skip [first tr, 3 ch, 1 dc, 3 ch], *1 DC in each of next 7 tr, 5 CH, skip [3 ch, 1 dc, 3 ch], repeat from *, ending 5 CH, 1 DC in 3rd of 6 ch, turn.

Row 7: 3 CH, skip [first dc, 2 ch], * [1 TR, 3 CH, 1 TR] in next ch, 3 CH, skip [2 ch, 2 dc], 1 DC in each of next 3 dc, 3 CH, skip [2 dc, 2 ch], repeat from *, ending [1 TR, 3 CH, 1 TR] in 3rd of 5 ch, turn.

Repeat rows 2–7.

Paddle stitch

A multiple of 8 sts + 2 (add 4 for foundation ch).

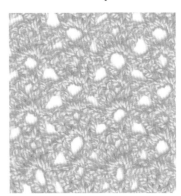

Row 1: [1 TR, 2 CH, 1 TR] in 7th ch from hook, *skip 3 ch, [2 TR, 1 CH, 2 TR] in next ch, skip 3 ch, [1 TR 2 CH, 1 TR] in next ch, repeat from * to last 7 ch, skip 3 ch, [2 TR, 1 CH, 2 TR] in next ch, skip 2 ch, 1 TR in last ch, turn.

Row 2: 3 CH, skip first 3 tr, * [1 TR, 2 CH, 1 TR] in 1 ch sp, skip 3 tr, [2 TR, 1 CH, 2 TR] in 2 ch sp, skip 3 tr, repeat from *, ending 1 TR in 6th of 6 ch, turn.

Repeat row 2, ending 1 TR in 3rd of 3 ch, turn.

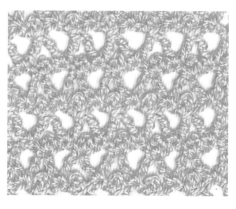

Picot triangles

A multiple of 4 sts + 1 (add 2 for foundation ch).

2

1

Special stitch – 1 PC (1 picot) = 3 CH, insert hook downwards through 3 front loops at top of group just worked and work 1 slip stitch.

Row 1: 1 DTR in 5th ch from hook, *3 CH, 2 DTR TOG, inserting hook first in same ch as previous dtr, then in following 4th ch, 1 PC, repeat from * to last 2 ch, 3 CH, 2 DTR TOG, inserting hook first in same ch as previous dtr, then in last ch, 1 PC, turn.

Row 2: 3 CH, skip [1 group, 1 pc, 1 ch], 1 DTR in next ch (the centre ch of 3), *3 CH, 2 DTR TOG, inserting hook first in same ch as previous dtr, then in 2nd of next 3 ch, 1 PC, repeat from *, ending 2 DTR TOG inserting hook first in same ch as last dtr, then in top of last dtr, 1 PC, turn. Repeat row 2.

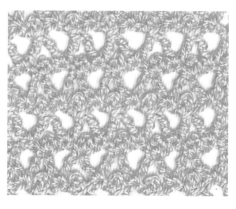 OPENWORK AND LACE STITCHES

5

Open scallops

A multiple of 8 sts + 1 (add 1 for foundation ch).

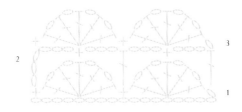

Row 1: Skip first 5 ch, *1 TR in next ch, [1 CH, 1 TR] 4 times in same ch as tr just made, skip 3 ch, 1 DC in next ch, skip 3 ch, repeat from *, ending 1 DC in last ch, turn.

Row 2: 6 CH, skip first dc, *skip [1 tr, 1 ch] twice, 1 DC in next tr (the centre tr of 5), 3 CH, skip [1 ch, 1 tr] twice, 1 TR in dc, 3 CH, repeat from *, ending 1 TR in ch after last tr, turn.

Row 3: 1 CH, skip first tr, *skip 3 ch, 1 TR in dc, [1 CH, 1 TR] 4 times in same dc as tr just made, skip 3 ch, 1 DC in tr, repeat from *, ending 1 DC in 3rd of 6 ch, turn.

Repeat rows 2 and 3.

STITCH KEY

○
chain

+
double crochet

⊤
treble

double treble

Special Stitch

3-chain picot

5

Bows and boxes

A multiple of 16 sts + 10 (add 2 for foundation ch).

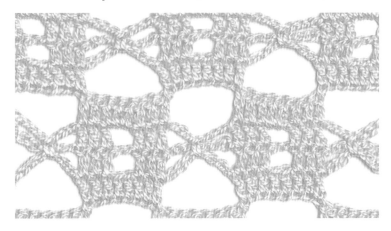

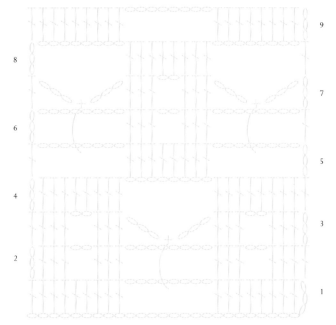

Row 1: 1 TR in 4th ch from hook, 1 TR in each of next 7 ch, *8 CH, skip 8 ch, 1 TR in each of next 8 ch, repeat from * to last ch, 1 TR in last ch, turn.

Row 2: 3 CH, skip first tr, 1 TR in each of next 3 tr, 2 CH, skip 2 tr, 1 TR in each of next 3 tr, *8 CH, skip 8 ch, 1 TR in each of next 3 tr, 2 CH, skip 2 tr, 1 TR in each of next 3 tr, repeat from *, ending 1 TR in 3rd of 3 ch, turn.

Row 3: 3 CH, skip first tr, 1 TR in each of next 3 tr, 2 CH, skip 2 ch, 1 TR in each of next 3 tr, *3 CH, 1 DC in 8 ch sp, 2 rows below (so catching both lengths of ch together), 3 CH, 1 TR in each of next 3 tr, 2 CH, skip 2 ch, 1 TR in each of next 3 tr, repeat from *, ending 1 TR in 3rd of 3 ch, turn.

Row 4: 3 CH, skip first tr, 1 TR in each of next 3 tr, 2 TR in 2 ch sp, 1 TR in each of next 3 tr, *8 CH, skip [3 ch, 1 dc, 3 ch], 1 TR in each of next 3 tr, 2 TR in 2 ch sp, 1 TR in each of next 3 tr, repeat from *, ending 1 TR in 3rd of 3 ch, turn.

Row 5: 11 CH, skip first 9 tr, *1 TR in each of next 8 ch, 8 CH, skip 8 tr, repeat from *, ending 1 TR in 3rd of 3 ch, turn.

Row 6: 11 CH, skip [first tr, 8 ch], *1 TR in each of next 3 tr, 2 CH, skip 2 tr, 1 TR in each of next 3 tr, 8 CH, skip 8 ch, repeat from *, ending 1 TR in 3rd of 11 ch, turn.

Row 7: 6 CH, 1 DC in 8 ch sp 2 rows below, 3 CH, *1 TR in each of next 3 tr, 2 CH, skip 2 ch, 1 TR in each of next 3 tr, 3 CH, 1 DC in 8 ch sp 2 rows below, 3 CH, repeat from *, ending 1 TR in 3rd of 11 ch, turn.

Row 8: 11 CH, skip [first tr, 3 ch, 1 dc, 3 ch], *1 TR in each of next 3 tr, 2 TR in 2 ch sp, 1 TR in each of next 3 tr, 8 CH, skip [3 ch, 1 dc, 3 ch], repeat from *, ending 1 TR in 3rd of 6 ch, turn.

Row 9: 3 CH, skip first tr, 1 TR in each of 8 ch, *8 CH, skip 8 tr, 1 TR in each of 8 ch, repeat from *, ending 1 TR in 3rd of 3 ch, turn.

Repeat rows 2–9.

STITCH
KEY

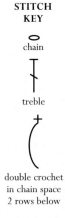

chain

treble

double crochet
in chain space
2 rows below

Sea stitch

A multiple of 12 sts + 1 (add 2 for foundation ch).

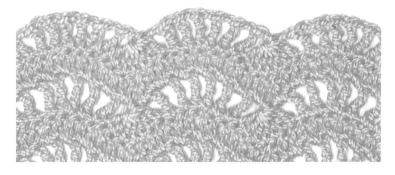

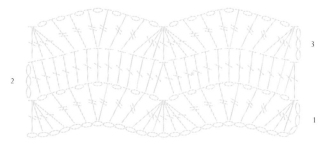

Row 1: 3 TR TOG over 4th, 5th and 6th ch from hook, *1 CH, [1 DTR in next ch, 1 CH] twice, [1 DTR, 1 CH, 1 DTR] in next ch, [1 CH, 1 DTR in next ch] twice, 1 CH, 7 TR TOG over next 7 ch, repeat from *, ending 4 TR TOG over last 4 ch, turn.

Row 2: 3 CH, skip first group, 1 TR in 1 ch sp, * [1 TR in dtr, 1 TR in 1 ch sp] 5 times, 1 TR in next dtr, 2 TR TOG, inserting hook in next 2 ch sps (skipping top of group), repeat from *, ending 2 TR TOG over last ch sp and top of last group, turn.

Row 3: 3 CH, skip top of group, 3 TR TOG over next 3 tr, *1 CH, [1 DTR in next tr, 1 CH] twice, [1 DTR, 1 CH, 1 DTR] in next tr, [1 CH, 1 DTR in next tr] twice, 1 CH, 7 TR TOG over next 7 sts, repeat from *, ending 4 TR TOG over last 4 dtr, turn.

Repeat rows 2 and 3.

Mophead stitch

A multiple of 10 sts + 1 (add 1 for foundation ch).

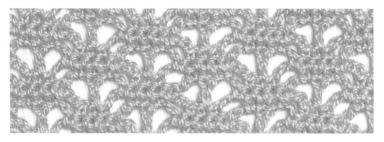

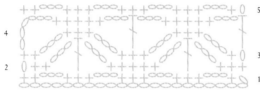

Row 1: 1 DC in 3rd ch from hook, *3 CH, skip 2 ch, 1 DC in each of next 3 ch, repeat from *, ending 1 DC in each of last 2 ch, turn.

Row 2: 1 CH, skip first dc, 1 DC in next dc, 1 DC in 3 ch sp, *3 CH, skip 1 dc, 1 TR in next dc (the centre dc of 3), 3 CH, skip 1 dc, 1 DC in 3 ch sp, 1 DC in each of next 3 dc, 1 DC in 3 ch sp, repeat from *, ending 1 DC in last 3 ch sp, 1 DC in last dc, 1 DC in 1 ch, turn.

Row 3: 1 CH, skip first dc, 1 DC in next dc, *3 CH, skip 1 dc, 1 DC in 3 ch sp, 1 DC in tr, 1 DC in 3 ch sp, 3 CH, skip 1 dc, 1 DC in each of next 3 dc (the centre 3 of 5), repeat from *, ending 1 DC in last dc, 1 DC in 1 ch, turn.

Row 4: 6 CH, skip first 2 dc, *1 DC in 3 ch sp, 1 DC in each of 3 dc, 1 DC in 3 ch sp, 3 CH, skip 1 dc, 1 TR in next dc (the centre dc of 3), 3 CH, skip 1 dc, repeat from *, ending 1 TR in 1 ch, turn.

Row 5: 1 CH, skip first tr, *1 DC in 3 ch sp, 3 CH, skip 1 dc, 1 DC in each of next 3 dc, (the centre 3 of 5), 3 CH, skip 1 dc, 1 DC in 3 ch sp, 1 DC in tr, repeat from *, ending 1 DC under 6 ch, 1 DC in 3rd of these 6 ch, turn. Repeat rows 2–5.

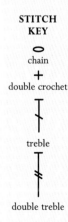

STITCH KEY

○ chain

+ double crochet

⊤ treble

⊤ double treble

Spider's web

A multiple of 14 sts + 1 (add 5 for foundation ch).

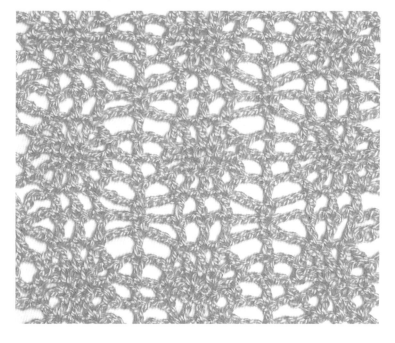

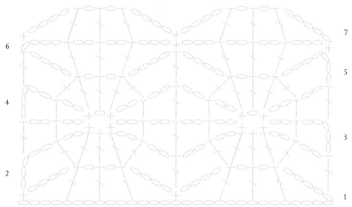

7

6

5

4

3

2

1

114

Row 1: Skip first 9 ch, *1 TR in next ch, [1 CH, skip 2 ch, 1 TR in next ch] twice, 4 CH, skip 3 ch, 1 DC in next ch, 4 CH, skip 3 ch, repeat from *, ending 1 DC in last ch, turn.

Row 2: 5 CH, skip 1 dc, *skip 4 ch, [1 TR, 2 CH, 1 TR] in next tr, skip 1 ch, 1 TR in next tr, skip 1 ch, [1 TR, 2 CH, 1 TR] in next tr, 2 CH, skip 4 ch, 1 TR in dc, 2 CH, repeat from *, ending 1 TR in 5th ch after last tr of previous row, turn.

Row 3: 5 CH, skip 1 tr, *skip 2 ch, 1 HTR in tr, 2 CH, skip 2 ch, 1 DC in tr, 1 SS in next tr, 1 DC in next tr, 2 CH, skip 2 ch, 1 HTR in tr, 2 CH, 1 TR in tr, 2 CH, repeat from *, ending 1 TR in 3rd of 5 ch, turn.

Row 4: 5 CH, skip first tr, *skip 2 ch, 1 HTR in htr, 2 CH, skip 2 ch, 1 DC in dc, 1 CH, skip 1 ss, 1 DC in dc, 2 CH, skip 2 ch, 1 HTR in htr, 2 CH, skip 2 ch, 1 TR in tr, 2 CH, repeat from *, ending 1 TR in 3rd of 5 ch, turn.

Row 5: 7 CH, skip first tr, * skip 2 ch, 2 TR TOG, inserting hook first in next htr, then in following dc, 1 CH, 1 TR in 1 ch sp, 1 CH, 2 TR TOG, inserting hook first in next dc, then in following htr, 4 CH, skip 2 ch, 1 TR in tr, 4 CH, repeat from *, ending 1 TR in 3rd of 5 ch, turn.

Row 6: 4 CH, skip first tr, *skip 4 ch, 1 TR in 2 tr tog, 2 CH, skip 1 ch, 1 TR in tr, 2 CH, skip 1 ch, 1 TR in 2 tr tog, 3 CH, skip 4 ch, 1 DC in tr, 3 CH, repeat from *, ending 1 DC in 3rd of 7 ch, turn.

Row 7: 5 CH, skip first dc, *skip 3 ch, 1 TR in next tr, [1 CH, skip 2 ch, 1 TR in tr] twice, 4 CH, skip 3 ch, 1 DC in dc, 4 CH, repeat from *, ending 1 DC in last ch, turn.

Repeat rows 2–7.

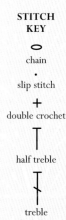

Little arcs

A multiple of 4 sts + 1 (add 3 for foundation ch).

Byzantine stitch

A multiple of 4 sts + 2 (add 2 for foundation ch).

3

2

1

2

1

Row 1: 1 DC in 4th ch from hook, *3 CH, 1 DC in next ch, 3 CH, skip 2 ch, 1 DC in next ch, repeat from * to end, turn.
Row 2: 3 CH, skip first dc, * [1 DC, 3 CH, 1 DC] in 3 ch sp, 3 CH, skip [1 dc, 3 ch, 1 dc], repeat from *, ending 1 DC under 3 ch, turn.
Repeat row 2.

Row 1: [1 DC, 3 CH, 1 DC] in 4th ch from hook, 1 DC in next ch, *2 CH, skip 2 ch, [1 DC, 3 CH, 1 DC] in next ch, 1 DC in next ch, repeat from * to last 3 ch, 2 CH, skip 2 ch, 1 DC in last ch, turn.
Row 2: 3 CH, skip first dc, *[1 TR, 3 CH, 1 DC in back loop only of tr just made, 1 TR] in 2 ch sp, 2 CH, skip 1 group, repeat from *, ending 1 TR under 3 ch, turn.
Row 3: 3 CH, skip first tr, work as row 2 from * to end.
Repeat row 3.

Crown stitch

A multiple of 7 sts + 2 (add 1 for foundation ch).

Row 1: 1 HTR in 3rd ch from hook, *3 CH, skip 2 ch, 1 DC in next ch, 3 CH, skip 2 ch, 1 HTR in each of next 2 ch, repeat from * to end, turn.

Row 2: 2 CH, skip first htr, 1 HTR in next htr, *3 CH, skip 3 ch, [1 DC, 3 CH, 1 DC] in dc, 3 CH, skip 3 ch, 1 HTR in each of 2 htr, repeat from *, working last HTR in 2nd of 2 ch, turn.

Row 3: 1 CH, skip first htr, 1 DC in next htr, *1 DC in 3 ch sp, 5 CH, skip [1 dc, 3 ch, 1 dc], 1 DC in next 3 ch sp, 1 DC in each of 2 htr, repeat from *, working last DC in 2nd of 2 ch, turn.

Row 4: 1 CH, skip first dc, 1 DC in next dc, *skip 1 dc, 7 DC in 5 ch sp, skip 1 dc, 1 DC in each of next 2 dc, repeat from *, working last DC in 1 ch, turn.

Row 5: 2 CH, skip first dc, 1 HTR in next dc, *3 CH, skip 3 dc, 1 DC in next dc (the 4th of 7), 3 CH, skip 3 dc, 1 HTR in each of next 2 dc, repeat from *, working last HTR in 1 ch, turn. Repeat rows 2–5.

STITCH KEY

O
chain

+
double crochet

⊤
half treble

⊺
treble

⊼
double crochet in back loop only (page 30)

Ruby lace

A multiple of 8 sts (add 1 for foundation ch).

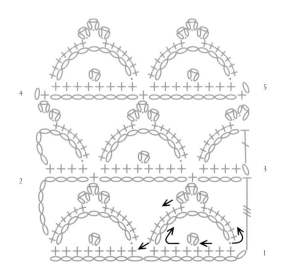

Special stitch – PC (picot) = 3 CH, 1 SS in first of these 3 ch.

Row 1: Skip first ch, *1 DC in each of next 4 ch, 1 PC, 1 DC in each of next 4 ch, turn, 9 CH, 1 SS in first dc of 8 just made, turn, [7 DC, 3 PC, 7 DC] in 9 ch sp, then continue along foundation ch: repeat from * to end, turn.

Row 2: 9 CH, skip [first 7 dc, 1 pc], 1 DC in centre of next pc, *8 CH, skip [1 pc, 14 dc, 1 pc], 1 DC in centre of next pc, repeat from *, ending 4 CH, skip [1 pc, last 7 dc], 1 TRTR in 1 ch at beginning previous row, turn.

Row 3: 1 CH, skip 1 trtr, 1 DC in each of first 4 ch, turn, 5 CH, 1 TR in 1 ch at beginning of row, turn, [2 PC, 7 DC] in 5 ch sp, then continue along previous row: *skip 1 dc, 1 DC in each of next 4 ch, 1 PC, 1 DC in each of next 4 ch, turn, 9 CH, 1 SS in first dc of 8 just made, turn, [7 DC, 3 PC, 7 DC] in 9 ch sp, repeat from *, ending skip 1 dc, 1 DC in each of first 4 ch of 9 ch at beginning previous row, turn, 8 CH, 1 SS in first dc of 4 just made, turn, [7 DC, 2 PC] in 8 ch sp, turn.

Row 4: 1 CH, 1 DC in centre of first pc, *8 CH, skip [1 pc, 14 dc, 1 pc], 1 DC in centre of next pc, repeat from * to end, turn.

Row 5: As row 1, skipping the dcs worked into pcs on previous row.

Repeat rows 2–5.

TIP

As a variation, you can omit the picots on rows 1, 3 and 5. Alternatively, work these single picots with 5 chains instead of 3.

STITCH KEY

o
chain

.
slip stitch

+
double crochet

treble

triple treble

←
direction of work

Special Stitch

3-chain picot

Daisy lace

A multiple of 8 sts + 1 (add 3 for foundation ch).

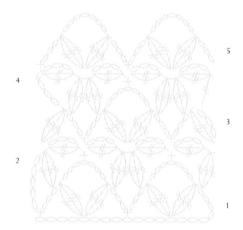

Row 1: 3 DTR TOG in 8th ch from hook, 7 CH, 3 DTR TOG in same ch as last group, 3 CH, skip 3 ch, 1 DC in next ch, *3 CH, skip 3 ch, [3 DTR TOG, 7 CH, 3 DTR TOG] in next ch, 3 CH, skip 3 ch, 1 DC in next ch, repeat from * to end, turn.

Row 2: 5 CH, skip [first dc, 2 ch], 3 DTR TOG in next ch, 3 CH, 2 DTR TOG in top of last group made, skip [1 group, 3 ch], *1 DC in next ch (the 4th of 7), 3 CH, 8 DTR TOG, inserting hook as follows: twice in dc just made, skip [3 ch, 1 group], insert 3 times in next ch, skip [2 ch, 1 dc, 2 ch], insert 3 times in next ch; 3 CH, 2 DTR TOG in top of last group made, skip [1 group, 3 ch], repeat from *, ending 1 DC in 4th of last 7 ch, 3 CH, 5 DTR TOG, inserting hook as follows: twice in last dc made, skip [3 ch, 1 group], insert 3 times in next ch; turn.

Row 3: 3 CH, 2 DTR TOG in top of first group, *3 CH, skip 3 ch, 1 DC in next dc, 3 CH, skip 3 ch, [3 DTR TOG, 7 CH, 3 DTR TOG] in top of next group, repeat from *, ending 3 CH, skip 3 ch, 3 DTR TOG in top of last group, turn.

Row 4: 7 CH, 8 DTR TOG, inserting hook as follows: twice in 4th ch from hook, skip [3 ch, 1 group], insert 3 times in next ch, skip [2 ch, 1 dc, 2 ch], insert 3 times in next ch; 3 CH, 2 DTR TOG in top of last group made, skip [1 group, 3 ch], *1 DC in next ch (the 4th of 7), 3 CH, 8 DTR TOG, inserting hook as follows: twice in last dc made, skip [3 ch, 1 group], insert 3 times in next ch, skip [2 ch, 1 dc, 2 ch], insert 3 times in next ch; 3 CH, 2 DTR TOG in top of last group made, skip [1 group, 3 ch], repeat from *, ending 1 DTR in 3rd of 3 ch, turn.

Row 5: 3 CH, skip first dtr, *skip 3 ch, [3 DTR TOG, 7 CH, 3 DTR TOG] in top of next group, 3 CH, skip 3 ch, 1 DC in next dc, repeat from *, working last DC in 4th of 7 ch, turn. Repeat rows 2–5.

Cornflower stitch

A multiple of 10 sts + 1 (add 1 for foundation ch).

Row 1: skip first 5 ch, * [1 TR, 1 CH, 1 TR] in next ch, 1 CH, 1 TR in next ch, 1 CH, [1 TR, 1 CH, 1 TR] in next ch, skip 3 ch, 1 DC in next ch, skip 3 ch, repeat from *, ending 1 DC in last ch, turn.

Row 2: 4 CH, 1 TR in first dc, *1 CH, skip [1 tr, 1 ch, 1 tr], 1 DC in 1 ch sp, 1 DC in tr, 1 DC in 1 ch sp, 1 CH, skip [1 tr, 1 ch, 1 tr], [1 TR, 3 CH, 1 TR] in next dc, repeat from *, ending [1 TR, 1 CH, 1 TR] in 1 ch, turn.

Row 3: 4 CH, skip first tr, [1 TR, 1 CH, 1 TR] in first 1 ch sp, *skip [1 tr, 1 ch, 1 dc], 1 DC in next dc, skip [1 dc, 1 ch, 1 tr], 1 TR in next 3 ch sp, [1 CH, 1 TR] 4 times in same 3 ch sp, repeat from *, ending 1 TR under 4 ch, [1 CH, 1 TR] twice under same 4 ch, turn.

Row 4: 1 CH, skip first tr, 1 DC in 1 ch sp, * 1 CH, skip [1 tr, 1 ch, 1 tr], [1 TR, 3 CH, 1 TR] in next dc, 1 CH, skip [1 tr, 1 ch, 1 tr], 1 DC in 1 ch sp, 1 DC in tr, 1 DC in 1 ch sp, repeat from *, ending 1 DC under 4 ch, 1 DC in 3rd of these 4 ch, turn.

Row 5: 1 CH, skip first dc, *skip [1 dc, 1 ch, 1 tr], 1 TR in next 3 ch sp, [1 CH, 1 TR] 4 times in same 3 ch sp, skip [1 tr, 1 ch, 1 dc], 1 DC in next dc, repeat from *, working last DC in 1 ch, turn.
Repeat rows 2–5.

TIP

Try working this stitch in two-row stripes, changing colours at the end of every right-side row.

STITCH KEY

o
chain

+
double crochet

T
treble

Openwork and Lace Stitches

Fancy lozenge stitch

A multiple of 8 sts + 1 (add 5 for foundation ch).

Row 1: 1 DC in 10th ch from hook, *4 CH, skip 3 ch, 1 DC in next ch, repeat from * to end, turn.

Row 2: 3 CH, skip first dc, *4 TR in 4 ch sp, 2 CH, skip 1 dc, 1 DC in next 4 ch sp, 2 CH, skip 1 dc, repeat from *, ending 1 TR in 5th ch from last dc of previous row, turn.

Row 3: 1 CH, skip first tr, *1 DC in 2 ch sp, 4 CH, skip 1 dc, 1 DC in next 2 ch sp, 4 CH, skip 4 tr, repeat from *, ending 1 DC in 3rd of 3 ch, turn.

Row 4: 5 CH, skip first dc, *1 DC in 4 ch sp, 2 CH, skip 1 dc, 4 TR in next 4 ch sp, 2 CH, skip 1 dc, repeat from *, ending 4 TR in last 4 ch sp, skip 1 dc, 1 TR in 1 ch, turn.

Row 5: 1 CH, skip first tr, *4 CH, skip 4 tr, 1 DC in 2 ch sp, 4 CH, skip 1 dc, 1 DC in next 2 ch sp, repeat from *, working last DC in 3rd of 5 ch, turn.

Repeat rows 2–5.

Trims and Edgings

A trim is a length of crochet worked separately from the main piece and then stitched either along an edge or in any position required. Crochet trims may also be stitched onto fabric. An edging is worked directly onto the edge of a main piece of crochet, often using a hook one or two sizes smaller than the main-piece hook.

Corded edging (Crab stitch)

Any number of sts.

STITCH KEY

o
chain

+
double crochet

T
treble

↱
do not turn

←
work right to left

→
work left to right

Special stitch – REV DC (reverse double crochet) = working from left to right, insert hook in next st to right, yrh, pull loop through, yrh, pull through both loops on hook.

With right side of work facing, join yarn at right of required edge.
Row 1: 1 CH, 1 DC in each st (or position) to end, do not turn.
Row 2: 1 CH, skip first dc, 1 REV DC in each dc, ending 1 REV DC in 1 ch. Fasten off.

6

Shell edging

A multiple of 4 sts + 1

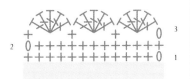

With right side of work facing, join yarn at right of required edge.

Row 1: 1 CH, 1 DC in each st (or position) to end, turn.

Row 2: 1 CH, skip first dc, 1 DC in each dc, ending 1 DC in 1 ch, turn.

Row 3: 1 CH, skip first dc, *skip 1 dc, 5 TR in next dc, skip 1 dc, 1 DC in next dc, repeat from *, ending 1 DC in 1 ch. Fasten off.

Block edging

A multiple of 4 sts

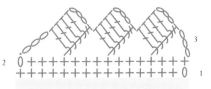

With right side of work facing, join yarn at right of required edge.

Row 1: 1 CH, 1 DC in each st (or position) to end, turn.

Row 2: 1 CH, skip first dc, 1 DC in each dc, ending 1 DC in 1 ch, turn.

Row 3: 3 CH, skip first 3 dc, *1 TR in next dc, 3 CH, [1 TR around stem of previous tr] 4 times in same place, skip next 3 dc, repeat from *, ending 3 CH, skip 3 dc, 1 SS in 1 ch. Fasten off.

Picot edging

Odd number of sts

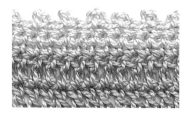

With right side of work facing, join yarn at right of required edge.

Row 1: 1 CH, 1 DC in each st (or position) to end, turn.

Row 2: 1 CH, skip first dc, 1 DC in each dc, ending 1 DC in 1 ch, turn.

Row 3: 1 CH, skip first dc, *3 CH, 1 SS in first of these 3 ch, skip 1 dc, 1 DC in next dc, repeat from * to end, working last DC in 1 ch. Fasten off.

Large picot edging

A multiple of 3 sts + 2

With right side of work facing, join yarn at right of required edge.

Row 1: 1 CH, 1 DC in each st (or position) to end, turn.

Row 2: 1 CH, skip first dc, 1 DC in each dc, ending 1 DC in 1 ch, turn.

Row 3: 1 CH, skip first dc, 1 DC in next dc, *5 CH, 1 SS in first of these 5 ch, skip 1 dc, 1 DC in each of next 2 dc, repeat from * to end, working last DC in 1 ch. Fasten off.

Crown picot edging

A multiple of 5 sts

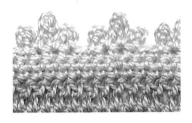

With right side of work facing, join yarn at right of required edge.

Row 1: 1 CH, 1 DC in each st (or position) to end, turn.

Row 2: 1 CH, skip first dc, 1 DC in each dc, ending 1 DC in 1 ch, turn.

Row 3: 1 CH, skip first dc, *[1 DC, 5 CH, 1 SS] in next dc, [1 DC, 7 CH, 1 SS] in next dc, [1 DC, 5 CH, 1 SS] in next dc, 1 DC in each of next 2 dc, repeat from *, ending 1 DC in 1 ch. Fasten off.

Blanket edging

A multiple of 4 sts + 3 (or as required).

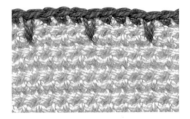

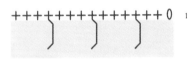

With right side of work facing, join yarn at right of required edge.

Row 1: 1 CH, 1 DC in each of first 2 sts (or positions), *1 DC, inserting hook about ¼ in. (6mm) below, 1 DC in each of next 3 sts (or positions), repeat from * to end. Fasten off.

Spikes may be made to any depth to suit the stitch used for the main piece, and may be spaced apart by any number of dc, to suit the length of the edge.

Spray edging

A multiple of 4 sts + 1 (or as required).

Special stitch – SCL (spike cluster) = insert hook about ¼ in. (6mm) below last dc made, yrh, pull loop through, insert about ⅜ in. (9mm) below current position, yrh, pull loop through, insert about ¼ in. (6mm) below next position, yrh, pull loop through, yrh, pull through 4 loops on hook.

With right side of work facing, join yarn at right of required edge.

Row 1: 1 CH, 1 DC in first st (or position), *1 SCL, 1 DC in each of next 3 sts (or positions), repeat from *, ending 1 DC in each of last 2 sts (or positions). Fasten off.

Spikes may be made to any depth to suit the stitch used for the main piece, and clusters may be spaced apart by any number of dc, to suit the length of the edge.

STITCH KEY

○
chain
·
slip stitch
+
double crochet

double crochet in main piece below

Special Stitch

spike cluster

Droplets trim

May be worked to any length: first row is worked sideways.

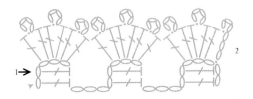

Row 1 (wrong side row): 5 CH, 1 TR in 4th ch from hook, 1 TR in next ch, *8 CH, 1 TR in 4th ch from hook, 1 TR in next ch, repeat from * until row 1 reaches length required, turn.

Row 2: 2 CH, skip 2 tr, 1 SS in 3 ch sp, 6 CH, 1 SS in 4th ch from hook, 1 TR in same 3 ch sp as first ss, [1 TR, 4 CH, 1 SS in first of these 4 ch, 1 TR] twice more in same 3 ch sp, *skip [2 ch at base of 2 tr of row 1, next 3 ch, 2 tr], then [1 TR, 4 CH, 1 SS in first of these 4 ch, 1 TR] 3 times in next 3 ch sp, repeat from * to end.

Fasten off.

TIP

Because the first row is worked sideways you can simply make it the length you require then work row 2 to complete the trim.

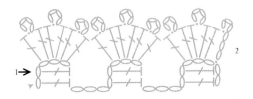

Blossom trim

May be worked to any length.

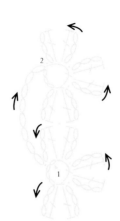

Row 1: 4 CH, 1 TR in 4th ch from hook (centre ring made), [3 CH, 2 TR into ring, 3 CH, 1 SS into ring] 3 times (3 petals made = 1 blossom), *11 CH, 1 TR in 4th ch from hook, 3 CH, 1 TR into ring, 1 SS between 2 tr of last petal made, 1 TR into ring, 3 CH, 1 SS into ring, [3 CH, 2 TR into ring, 3 CH, 1 SS into ring] twice, repeat from * to length required. Fasten off.

STITCH KEY

○
chain

•
slip stitch

treble

▶
starting point

↑
direction of work

3 chain picot

Double shell trim

May be worked to any length.

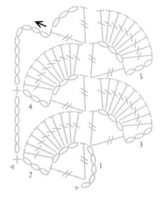

Row 1: 5 CH, [1 DTR, 3 CH, 1 DTR] in 5th ch from hook, turn.

Row 2: 3 CH, skip first dtr, 9 TR in 3 ch sp, skip 1 dtr, [1 DTR, 3 CH, 1 DTR] under 4 ch at beginning of row 1, turn.

Row 3: 3 CH, skip first dtr, 9 TR in 3 ch sp, skip 1 dtr, [1 DTR, 3 CH, 1 DTR] in sp before next tr, turn.

Repeat row 3 to length required, making an even number of rows in all. Do not turn.

Header row (optional): 9 CH, 1 DC in 3rd of 3 ch at beginning of shell of previous row, *6 CH, 1 DC in 3rd of 3 ch at beginning of next shell along this edge, repeat from * to end. Fasten off.

Petal trim

A multiple of 9 sts + 3.

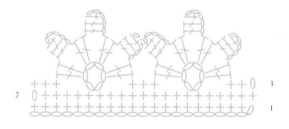

Row 1: 1 DC in 2nd ch from hook, 1 DC in each ch to end, turn.

Row 2: 1 CH, skip first dc, 1 DC in each of next 5 dc, *6 CH, 1 DC in each of next 9 dc, repeat from *, ending 1 DC in each of last 5 dc, 1 DC in 1 ch, turn.

Row 3: 1 CH, skip first dc, 1 DC in each of next 2 dc, skip 3 dc, [2 TR in 6 ch loop, 5 CH, 1 EXDC in 3rd ch from hook, 1 TR in each of next 2 ch] 3 times in same loop (3 petals made),

2 TR in same loop, skip 3 dc, 1 DC in each of next 3 dc, *skip 3 dc, 2 TR in 6 ch loop, 3 CH, 1 SS in 2 ch sp at tip of last petal made, 1 CH, 1 EXDC in 3rd st from hook, 1 TR in each of next 2 ch, [2 TR in 6 ch loop, 5 CH, 1 EXDC in 3rd ch from hook, 1 TR in each of next 2 ch] twice in same loop, 2 TR in same loop, skip 3 dc, 1 DC in each of next 3 dc, repeat from * to end, working last DC in 1 ch. Fasten off.

Coronet trim

A multiple of 7 sts + 1.

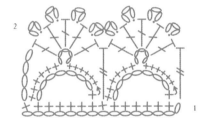

Row 1: 1 DC in 2nd ch from hook, 1 DC in each of next 5 ch, * turn, 7 CH, skip 5 dc, 1 DC in next dc, turn, [6 DC, 5 CH, 6 DC] in 7 ch sp, 1 DC in each of next 7 foundation ch, repeat from * ending 1 DC in last foundation ch, turn.

Row 2: 4 CH, skip first dc, *skip next 6 dc, [1 TR, 3 CH, 1 SS in first of these 3 ch] 4 times in 5 ch loop, 1 TR in same 5 ch loop, skip 6 dc, 1 DTR in next dc, repeat from * to end, working last DTR in 1 ch. Fasten off.

Cockleshell trim

May be worked to any length.

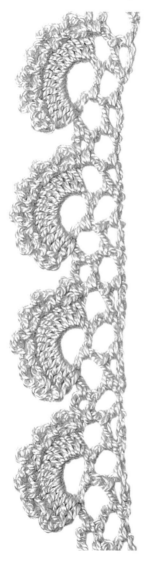

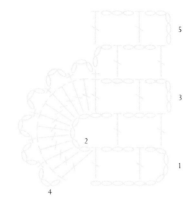

Row 1: 11 CH, 1 TR in 7th ch from hook, 3 CH, skip 3 ch, 1 TR in last ch, turn.

Row 2: 7 CH, skip first tr, 1 TR in 3 ch sp, 3 CH, skip 1 tr, 1 TR under 6 ch, turn.

Row 3: 5 CH, skip first tr, 1 TR in 3 ch sp, 3 CH, skip 1 tr, 13 TR under 7 ch, turn.

Row 4: 3 CH, skip first 2 tr, [1 DC in next tr, 3 CH, skip next tr] 5 times, 1 DC in next tr, 3 CH, 1 TR in 3 ch sp, 3 CH, 1 TR under 5 ch, turn.

Row 5: 5 CH, skip first tr, 1 TR in 3 ch sp, 3 CH, skip next tr, 1 TR under 3 ch, turn.

Repeat rows 2–5 to length required, ending row 4. Fasten off.

STITCH KEY

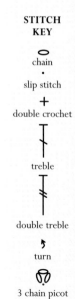

chain

slip stitch

double crochet

treble

double treble

turn

3 chain picot

Pansy trim

May be worked to any length.

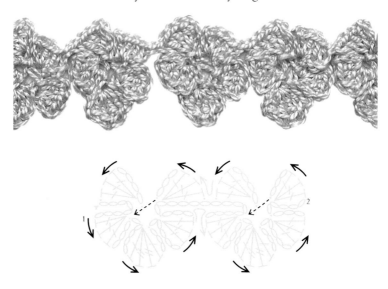

Row 1: On this row, 3 lower petals of each flower are worked: 8 CH, * [3 TR, 3 CH, 1 SS] in 4th ch from hook, 5 CH, [1 TR, 2 DTR, 1 TR, 3 CH, 1 SS] in 4th ch from hook, 5 CH, [3 TR, 3 CH, 1 SS] in 4th ch from hook, 14 CH, repeat from * to length required, ending last repeat with 5 CH only, do not turn.

Row 2: Rotate the work to continue along top edge, completing each flower: * skip 3 ch, [3 TR, 3 CH, 1 SS] in next ch, 1 SS in corresponding ch at base of first petal of this flower, 4 CH, 3 TR in 4th ch from hook, skip first 3 ch of 10 ch between flowers, 1 SS in each of next 2 ch, repeat from *, ending 1 SS in first ch made at beginning of first flower. Fasten off.

Clusters, Puffs and Bobbles

7

All these stitch patterns make bold, raised effects. Clusters, puffs and popcorns are normally groups of stitches joined together at both top and bottom. Bobbles are formed by working such stitch groups on a tight, firm background. Popcorns are joined at the top by linking the first stitch of the group to the last, making a cup shape. For bullion stitches the yarn is wound several times around the hook to form a coil.

Aligned treble clusters

Any number of sts (add 3 for foundation ch – work ch loosely).

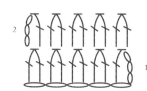

Row 1: 1 TR in 4th ch from hook, 2 TR TOG in each ch to end, turn.
Row 2: 3 CH, 1 TR in first 2 tr tog, 2 TR TOG in top of each 2 tr tog to end, turn.
Repeat row 2.

Alternate treble clusters

Odd number of sts (add 3 for foundation ch).

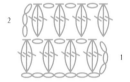

Row 1: 3 TR TOG all in 4th ch from hook, *1 CH, skip 1 ch, 3 TR TOG all in next ch, repeat from * to end, turn.
Row 2: 3 CH, skip first 3 tr tog, *3 TR TOG in next ch sp, 1 CH, skip next 3 tr tog, repeat from *, ending 3 TR TOG under 3 ch, turn.
Repeat row 2.

Pique stitch

Any number of sts (add 3 for foundation ch – work ch loosely).

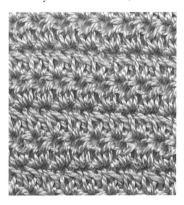

Special stitch – GP (group): 1 treble and 1 half treble worked together, as follows: yrh, insert hook in next st, yrh, pull loop through, yrh, pull through first 2 loops on hook, yrh, insert hook in same st as before, yrh, pull loop through, yrh, pull through all 4 loops on hook.
Row 1: 1 HTR in 4th ch from hook, 1 GP in each ch to end, turn.
Row 2: 3 CH, 1 HTR in first gp, 1 GP in each gp, ending 1 GP in 1 htr, turn.
Repeat row 2.

CLUSTERS, PUFFS AND BOBBLES

7

Large clusters

Even number of sts (add 2 for foundation ch).

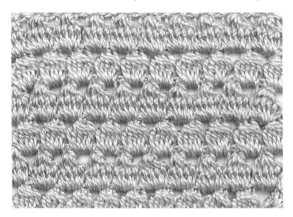

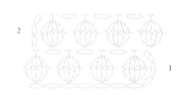

STITCH KEY

chain

half treble

3 trebles together in same place

Special Stitches

large cluster

1 treble together with 1 half treble

Special stitch – LC (large cluster): [yrh, insert hook as given, yrh, pull loop through, yrh, pull through 2 loops] 5 times in same place, yrh, pull through first 5 loops on hook, yrh, pull through both loops on hook.

Row 1: 1 LC in 4th ch from hook, *1 CH, skip 1 ch, 1 LC in next ch, repeat from * to end, turn.

Row 2: 3 CH, skip first lc, *1 LC in next ch sp, 1 CH, skip next lc, repeat from *, ending 1 LC under 3 ch, turn.

Repeat row 2.

Lace clusters

A multiple of 6 sts + 2 (add 3 for foundation ch).

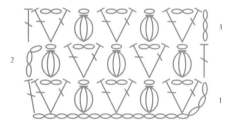

Special stitch – HTRC (half treble cluster): [yrh, insert hook as given, yrh, pull loop through] 4 times in same place, yrh, pull through all loops on hook, 1 CH to close the cluster.

Row 1: [1 TR, 2 CH, 1 TR] in 4th ch from hook, skip 2 ch, *1 HTRC in next ch, skip 2 ch, [1 TR, 2 CH, 1 TR] in next ch, repeat from * to last ch, 1 TR in last ch, turn.

Row 2: 3 CH, skip first 2 tr, *1 HTRC in 2 ch sp, skip 1 tr, [1 TR, 2 CH, 1 TR] in top of next htrc, skip 1 tr, repeat from *, ending 1 HTRC in last 2 ch sp, skip 1 tr, 1 TR in 3rd of 3 ch, turn.

Row 3: 3 CH, skip first tr, *[1 TR, 2 CH, 1 TR] in top of next htrc, skip 1 tr, 1 HTRC in 2 ch sp, skip 1 tr, repeat from *, ending 1 TR in 3rd of 3 ch, turn.

Repeat rows 2 and 3.

Honeycomb stitch

A multiple of 3 sts (add 1 for foundation ch).

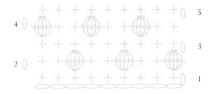

Special stitch – CL (cluster): 5 trebles together, all worked into same stitch.

Row 1: 1 DC in 2nd ch from hook, 1 DC in each ch to end, turn.

Row 2: 1 CH, 1 DC in each of first 2 dc, *1 CL in next dc, 1 DC in each of next 2 dc, repeat from *, ending 1 CL in last dc, turn.

Row 3: 1 CH, *1 DC in cl, 1 DC in each of next 2 dc, repeat from * to end, turn.

Row 4: 1 CH, 1 CL in first dc, *1 DC in each of next 2 dc, 1 CL in next dc, repeat from *, ending 1 DC in each of last 2 dc, turn.

Row 5: 1 CH, 1 DC in first dc, 1 DC in next dc, *1 DC in cl, 1 DC in each of next 2 dc, repeat from *, ending 1 DC in last cl, turn.

Repeat rows 2–5.

Clusters, Puffs and Bobbles

Ball stitch

A multiple of 4 sts + 3.

Row 1: 1 DC in 2nd ch from hook, 1 DC in each ch to end, turn.

Row 2: 1 CH, skip first dc, 1 DC in each of next 2 dc, *4 HTR TOG all in next dc, 1 DC in each of next 3 dc, repeat from * to end, working last DC in 1 ch, turn.

Row 3: 1 CH, skip first dc, 1 DC in each st to end, working last DC in 1 ch, turn.

Row 4: 1 CH, skip first dc, *4 HTR TOG all in next dc, 1 DC in each of next 3 dc, repeat from *, ending 1 DC in 1 ch, turn.

Row 5: As row 3.

Repeat rows 2–5.

Pineapple stitch

Even number of sts (add 2 for foundation ch).

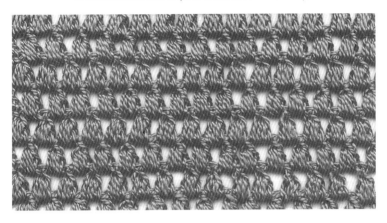

STITCH KEY

o
chain

+
double crochet

treble

4 half trebles
together in
same place

Special Stitches

pineapple stitch

Special stitch – PS (pineapple stitch): [yrh, insert hook as given, yrh, draw a loop through] 4 times in same place, yrh, draw through first 8 loops on hook, yrh, draw through remaining 2 loops on hook.

Row 1: 1 PS in 4th ch from hook, 1 CH, *skip 1 ch, 1 PS in next ch, 1 CH, repeat from * to last 2 ch, skip 1 ch, 1 TR in last ch, turn.

Row 2: 3 CH, skip first tr, 1 PS in first ch sp, *1 CH, skip 1 ps, 1 PS in next ch sp, repeat from *, ending 1 CH, skip 1 ps, 1 TR in 3rd of 3 ch, turn.
Repeat row 2.

Raised pineapple stitch

A multiple of 4 sts + 3.

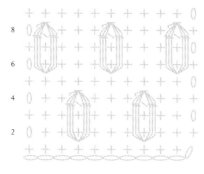

Special stitch – RPS (raised pineapple stitch): insert hook as given, yrh, pull loop through, [yrh, insert hook into same st 2 rows below, yrh, pull loop through, yrh, pull through first 2 loops on hook] 6 times, yrh, pull through all 8 loops on hook.

Row 1: 1 DC in 2nd ch from hook, 1 DC in each ch to end, turn.

Row 2: 1 CH, skip first dc, 1 DC in each dc, ending 1 DC in 1 ch, turn.

Row 3: As row 2.

Row 4: 1 CH, skip first dc, 1 DC in each of next 2 dc, *1 RPS in next dc, 1 DC in each of next 3 dc, repeat from * to end, working last DC in 1 ch, turn.

Row 5: 1 CH, skip first dc, 1 DC in each st, ending 1 DC in 1 ch, turn.

Row 6: As row 2.

Row 7: As row 2.

Row 8: 1 CH, skip first dc, *1 RPS in next dc, 1 DC in each of next 3 dc, repeat from *, ending 1 RPS in last dc, 1 DC in 1 ch, turn.

Row 9: As row 5.

Repeat rows 2–9.

Forked clusters

A multiple of 3 sts + 2 (add 3 for foundation ch).

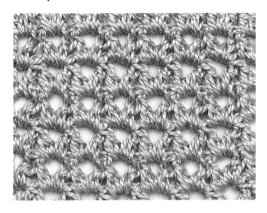

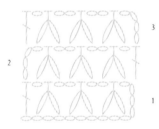

2

1

Special stitch – FC (forked cluster): *[yrh, insert hook at first position given, yrh, pull loop through] twice in same place, yrh, pull through first 4 loops on hook, repeat from * at second position given, yrh, pull through all 3 loops on hook.

Row 1: 1 FC, inserting hook in 5th and 7th ch from hook, *2 CH, 1 FC, inserting hook in next ch and following alternate ch, repeat from * to last ch, 1 CH, 1 TR in last ch, turn.

Row 2: 4 CH, skip first tr, 1 FC, inserting hook in first and 2nd ch sps, *2 CH, 1 FC, inserting hook in same ch sp as last insertion, then in next ch sp, repeat from *, ending under 4 ch, 1 CH, 1 TR under same 4 ch, turn.

Repeat row 2.

STITCH KEY

Special Stitches

forked cluster

raised pineapple stitch

145

Twin clusters

A multiple of 3 sts + 2.

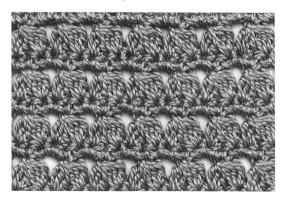

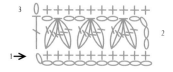

Special stitch – TC (twin cluster): [yrh, insert hook in next dc, yrh, pull loop through, yrh, pull through first 2 loops on hook] 3 times in same place, skip next dc, repeat [to] 3 times in next dc, yrh, pull through all 7 loops on hook.

Row 1 (wrong side row): 1 DC in 2nd ch from hook, 1 DC in each ch to end, turn.

Row 2: 4 CH, skip first dc, *1 TC over next 3 dc, 2 CH, repeat from *, ending 1 TC over last 3 dc, 1 CH, 1 TR in 1 ch, turn.

Row 3: 1 CH, skip first tr, 1 DC in 1 ch sp, *1 DC in top of tc, 2 DC in 2 ch sp, repeat from *, ending 1 DC in top of last tc, 1 DC under 4 ch, 1 DC in 3rd of these 4 ch, turn.

Repeat rows 2 and 3.

Raised forked clusters

A multiple of 6 sts + 1 (add 2 for foundation ch).

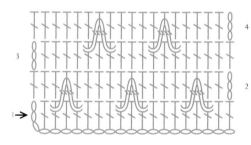

Special stitch – RFC (raised forked cluster): *[yrh, insert hook from right to left around stem of tr below previous tr, yrh, pull loop through, yrh, pull through first 2 loops on hook], twice in same place, yrh, pull through first 2 loops on hook*, skip 1 tr, repeat from * to * around stem of next tr, yrh, pull through all 3 loops on hook.

Row 1 (wrong side row): 1 TR in 4th ch from hook, 1 TR in each ch to end, turn.

Row 2: 3 CH, skip first tr, 1 TR in each of next 2 tr, *1 RFC, 1 TR in 3rd tr used for rfc, 1 TR in each of next 4 tr, repeat from *, ending 1 TR in each of last 2 tr, 1 TR in 3rd of 3 ch, turn.

Row 3: 3 CH, skip first tr, 1 TR in each st, ending 1 TR in 3rd of 3 ch, turn.

Row 4: 3 CH, skip first tr, 1 TR in each of next 5 tr, *1 RFC, 1 TR in 3rd tr used for rfc, 1 TR in each of next 4 tr, repeat from *, ending 1 TR in 3rd of 3 ch, turn.

Row 5: As row 3.
Repeat rows 2–5.

STITCH KEY

o
chain

+
double crochet

treble

Special Stitches

raised forked cluster

twin cluster

Bead stitch

Even number of sts.

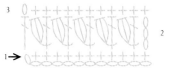

Special stitch – SCL (slanting cluster): [yrh, insert hook around stem of previous tr from right to left, yrh, pull loop through] 3 times in same place, yrh, pull through first 6 loops on hook, yrh, pull through both loops on hook.
Row 1 (wrong side row): 1 DC in 2nd ch from hook, 1 DC in each ch to end, turn.
Row 2: 3 CH, skip first dc, *1 TR in next dc, 1 SCL , skip 1 dc, repeat from *, ending 1 TR in 1 ch, turn.
Row 3: 1 CH, skip first tr, *1 DC in scl, 1 DC in tr, repeat from *, ending 1 DC in 3rd of 3 ch, turn.
Repeat rows 2 and 3.

Boxed beads

A multiple of 3 sts + 1 (add 1 for foundation ch).

Special stitch – SCL (slanting cluster): As for Bead stitch, left.
Row 1 (wrong side row): 1 DC in 3rd ch from hook, 1 DC in next ch, *1 EXDC in next ch, 1 DC in each of next 2 ch, repeat from *, ending 1 EXDC in last ch, turn.
Row 2: 2 CH, skip first exdc, *1 TR in next dc, 1 SCL, skip next dc, 1 EXDC in exdc, repeat from *, working last EXDC in 2nd of 2 ch, turn.
Row 3: 2 CH, skip first exdc, *1 DC in scl, 1 DC in tr, 1 EXDC in exdc, repeat from *, working last EXDC in 2nd of 2 ch, turn.
Repeat rows 2 and 3.

CLUSTERS, PUFFS AND BOBBLES

Bullion stitch

A multiple of 6 sts + 5.

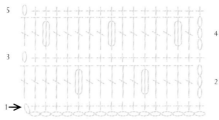

Special stitch – BS (bullion stitch): yrh 7 times, insert hook, yrh, pull loop through, yrh, pull through all 9 loops on hook.

Row 1 (wrong side row): 1 DC in 2nd ch from hook, 1 DC in each ch to end, turn.

Row 2: 3 CH, skip first dc, 1 TR in each of next 4 dc, *1 BS in next dc, 1 TR in each of next 5 dc, repeat from * to end, working last TR in 1 ch, turn.

Row 3: 1 CH, skip first tr, 1 DC in each of next 4 tr, *1 DC in bs, 1 DC in each of next 5 tr, repeat from *, working last DC in 3rd of 3 ch, turn.

Row 4: 3 CH, skip first dc, 1 TR in next dc, *1 BS in next dc, 1 TR in each of next 5 dc, repeat from *, ending 1 TR in last dc, 1 TR in 1 ch, turn.

Row 5: 1 CH, skip first tr, 1 DC in next tr, *1 DC in bs, 1 DC in each of next 5 tr, repeat from *, ending 1 DC in last tr, 1 DC in 3rd of 3 ch, turn.
Repeat rows 2–5.

Clusters, Puffs and Bobbles

7

Alternate popcorns

A multiple of 4 sts (add 3 for foundation ch).

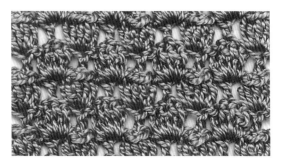

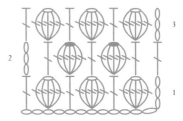

Special stitch – RSP (popcorn on right side row): Work 5 TR all in next st, withdraw hook leaving a loop, reinsert hook under back loop only of first of these 5 tr, catch empty loop and pull it through to close the popcorn.

Special stitch – WSP (popcorn on wrong side row): As RSP, but to close reinsert hook from top of first of 5 tr, down under front loop only.

Row 1: 1 RSP in 5th ch from hook, skip 1 ch, 1 TR in next ch, *skip 1 ch, 1 RSP in next ch, skip 1 ch, 1 TR in next ch, repeat from * to end, turn.

Row 2: 3 CH, skip first tr, *1 TR in rsp, 1 WSP in tr, repeat from *, ending 1 TR in last rsp, 1 TR in next ch, turn.

Row 3: 3 CH, skip first tr, *1 RSP in next tr, 1 TR in wsp, repeat from *, ending 1 RSP in last tr, 1 TR in next ch, turn.

Repeat rows 2 and 3.

Paired popcorns

A multiple of 6 sts + 1.

Special stitch – PC (popcorn): 5 TR in same stitch, withdraw hook leaving a loop, reinsert hook under two threads at top of first of these 5 tr, catch empty loop and pull it through to close the popcorn.

Row 1 (wrong side row): 1 DC in 2nd ch from hook, *1 CH, skip 1 ch, 2 DC in next ch, 1 CH, skip 1 ch, 1 DC in each of next 3 ch, repeat from *, ending 1 DC in each of last 2 ch, turn.

Row 2: 3 CH, skip first dc, 1 TR in next dc, *skip 1 ch, 1 PC in next dc, 1 CH, 1 PC in next dc, skip 1 ch, 1 TR in each of next 3 dc, repeat from *, ending 1 TR in last dc, 1 TR in 1 ch, turn.

Row 3: 1 CH, skip first tr, 1 DC in next tr, *1 CH, skip 1 pc, 2 DC in next 1 ch sp, 1 CH, skip 1 pc, 1 DC in each of next 3 tr, repeat from *, ending 1 DC in last tr, 1 DC in 3rd of 3 ch, turn.

Repeat rows 2 and 3.

7

CLUSTERS, PUFFS AND BOBBLES

Raised popcorns

A multiple of 6 sts + 5.

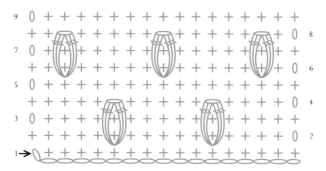

Special stitch – 1 RP (raised popcorn): 1 CH, 6 TR all into dc 2 rows below next dc, withdraw hook leaving a loop, reinsert hook into ch worked before 6 tr, catch empty loop and pull it through to close the popcorn.

Row 1 (wrong side row): 1 DC in 2nd ch from hook, 1 DC in each ch to end, turn.

Row 2: 1 CH, skip first dc, 1 DC in each dc, ending 1 DC in 1 ch, turn.

Row 3: As row 2.

Row 4: 1 CH, skip first dc, 1 DC in each of next 4 dc, *1 RP in dc 2 rows below next dc, 1 DC in each of next 5 dc, repeat

---

152

from * to end, working last DC in 1 ch, turn.

Row 5: 1 CH, skip first dc, 1 DC in each st, ending 1 DC in 1 ch, turn.

Row 6: As row 2.

Row 7: As row 2.

Row 8: 1 CH, skip first dc, 1 DC in next dc, *1 RP in dc 2 rows below next dc, 1 DC in each of next 5 dc, repeat from *, ending 1 DC in last dc, 1 DC in 1 ch, turn.

Row 9: As row 5.

Repeat rows 2–9.

Spot stitch

A multiple of 4 sts + 1.

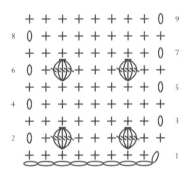

STITCH KEY

o
chain

+
double crochet

5 trebles together in same place

Special Stitches

six treble raised popcorn

Row 1: 1 DC in 2nd ch from hook, 1 DC in each ch to end, turn.

Row 2 (wrong side row): 1 CH, skip first dc, 1 DC in next dc, *5 TR TOG all in next dc, 1 DC in each of next 3 dc, repeat from *, ending 1 DC in last dc, 1 DC in 1 ch, turn.

Row 3: 1 CH, skip first dc, 1 DC in each st to end, turn.

Row 4: As row 3.

Row 5: As row 3

Repeat rows 2–5.

8 Spike Stitches

A spike stitch is created when the hook is inserted some distance away from the usual position, either in a lower row or to one side. Sometimes an elongated stitch is formed across the surface of the work, as seen in basket stitch and cable stitch. At other times the effect is to distort the previous row, as in alternate spike stitch. Spike stitches are usually drawn up rather loosely to the height of the working row.

Alternate spike stitch

Even number of sts.

Special stitch – 1 DC BELOW: 1 DC in base of next dc.

Row 1: 1 DC in 2nd ch from hook, 1 DC in each ch to end, turn.

Row 2: 1 CH, skip first dc, *1 DC in next dc, 1 DC BELOW following dc, repeat from *, ending 1 DC in 1 ch, turn.

Repeat row 2.

Basket stitch

A multiple of 4 sts + 3.

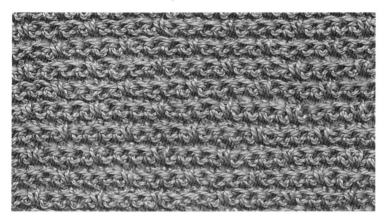

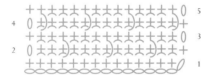

Special stitch – 1 DC BELOW: As for Alternate spike stitch (see page 154).

Row 1: 1 DC in 2nd ch from hook, 1 DC in each ch to end, turn.

Row 2: 1 CH, skip first dc, 1 DC in back loop of each dc, ending 1 DC in 1 ch, turn.

Row 3: 1 CH, skip first dc, 1 DC in back loop of each of next 2 dc, *1 DC BELOW, 1 DC in back loop of each of next 3 dc, repeat from * to end, working last DC in 1 ch, turn.

Row 4: As row 2.

Row 5: 1 CH, skip first dc, *1 DC BELOW next dc, 1 DC in back loop of each of next 3 dc, repeat from *, ending 1 DC BELOW last dc, 1 DC in 1 ch, turn.

Repeat rows 2–5.

STITCH KEY

◯
chain

+
double crochet

ᚐ
double crochet in back loop only

Special Stitches

ʃ
double crochet below

Cable stitch

A multiple of 4 sts + 2.

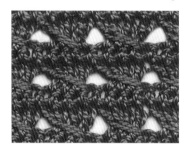

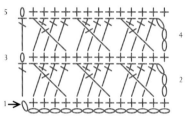

Special stitch – 1 CABLE ST: Work 1 TR, inserting hook 4 sts to the right in last dc skipped.

Row 1 (wrong side row): 1 DC in 2nd ch from hook, 1 DC in each ch to end, turn.

Row 2: 3 CH, skip first dc, *skip next dc, 1 TR in each of next 3 dc, 1 CABLE ST, repeat from *, ending 1 TR in 1 ch, turn.

Row 3: 1 CH, skip first tr, 1 DC in each tr, ending 1 DC in 3rd of 3 ch, turn.

Repeat rows 2 and 3. The cables should form vertical rows.

Open ridge stitch

Even number of sts.

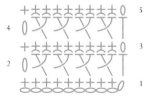

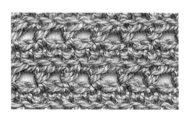

Row 1: 1 DC in 2nd ch from hook, 1 DC in each ch to end, turn.

Row 2: 1 CH, skip first dc, *skip 1 dc, 1 HTR in next dc, 1 HTR in sp between last 2 sts worked, repeat from *, ending 1 HTR in 1 ch, turn.

Row 3: 1 CH, skip first htr, 1 DC in back loop of each htr, ending 1 DC in 1 ch, turn. Repeat rows 2 and 3.

Spiked boxes

Even number of sts (add 3 for foundation ch).

STITCH
KEY

O
chain

+
double crochet

T
treble

ㅗ
double crochet
in back loop
only

T
half treble

⌐
half treble
between last
2 stitches
worked

ᐱ
2 half treble
together

**Special
Stitches**

spike treble in
row below

cable stitch

Special stitch – SPIKE TR:
Work 1 TR, inserting hook in
row below in sp between the 2
sts last worked into.

Row 1: 2 HTR TOG over 4th
and 5th ch from hook, *1 TR in
same ch as last st, 2 HTR TOG
over next 2 ch, repeat from * to
end, turn.

Row 2: 3 CH, 2 HTR TOG over
first 2 htr tog and next tr, *1
SPIKE TR, 2 HTR TOG over

next 2 htr tog and following tr,
repeat from *, ending 2 HTR
TOG over last 2 htr tog and 3rd
of 3 ch, turn.

Row 3: 3 CH, 2 HTR TOG over
first 2 htr tog and next spike tr,
*1 SPIKE TR, 2 HTR TOG over
next 2 htr tog and following
spike tr, repeat from *, ending 2
HTR TOG over last 2 htr tog
and 3rd of 3 ch, turn.
Repeat row 3.

Diagonal spike stitch

A multiple of 4 sts + 2 (add 2 for foundation ch).

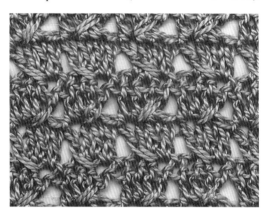

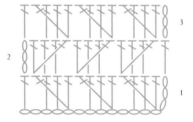

Special stitch – SPIKE TR: 1 TR in same place as first of 3 previous tr.

Row 1: 1 TR in 4th ch from hook, 1 TR in each of next 2 ch, 1 SPIKE TR in same place as first tr, *skip 1 ch, 1 TR in each of next 3 ch, 1 SPIKE TR, repeat from * to last 2 ch, skip 1 ch, 1 TR in last ch, turn.

Row 2: 3 CH, skip first tr, *1 TR in spike tr, 1 TR in each of next 2 tr, 1 SPIKE TR, skip 1 tr, repeat from *, ending 1 TR in 3rd of 3 ch, turn.
Repeat row 2.

Small daisy stitch

Even number of sts (add 3 for foundation ch).

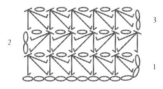

Special stitch – DAISY CL: insert hook in st closing previous daisy cl, yrh, pull through a loop, insert hook in same place as last spike of previous daisy cl, yrh, pull through a loop, skip 1 ch, insert hook in next st, yrh, pull through a loop, yrh, pull through 4 loops on hook.

Row 1: Make first DAISY CL in same way as above, but inserting hook in 2nd, 3rd, and 5th ch from hook, * 1 CH, 1 DAISY CL, repeat from * to end, turn.

Row 2: 3 CH, make first DAISY CL by inserting hook in 2nd and 3rd ch from hook, then skip [first daisy cl, 1 ch], make third insertion in top of next daisy cl, * 1 CH, 1 DAISY CL, repeat from * to end, turn.

Repeat row 2.

○
chain

┬
treble

Special Stitches

↖
daisy cluster

⤲
spike treble

Brick stitch

A multiple of 4 sts + 1 (add 2 for foundation ch).

Special stitch – TR BELOW (treble below): 1 TR in empty loop of tr 1 row below next st.

Row 1: 1 TR in 4th ch from hook, 1 TR in each ch to end, turn.

Row 2: 1 CH, skip first tr, 1 DC in front loop of each tr, ending 1 DC in 3rd of 3 ch, turn.

Row 3: 3 CH, skip first dc, *1 TR BELOW next dc, 1 TR in each of next 3 dc, repeat from * to end, working last TR in 1 ch, turn.

Row 4: As row 2.

Row 5: 3 CH, skip first dc, 1 TR in each of next 2 dc, *1 TR BELOW next dc, 1 TR in each of next 3 dc, repeat from *, ending 1 TR BELOW last dc, 1 TR in 1 ch, turn.

Repeat rows 2–5.

Treble crosses

A multiple of 6 sts + 5 (add 2 for foundation ch).

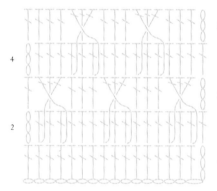

STITCH KEY

o chain

+ double crochet

T treble

♣ double crochet in front loop only

Special Stitches

treble cross

treble below

Special stitch – TR CR (treble cross): Skip next 2 tr, 1 TR in same place as base of next tr, 1 TR in second of 2 skipped tr, 1 TR in same place as base of first skipped tr.

Row 1: 1 TR in 4th ch from hook, 1 TR in each ch to end, turn.

Row 2: 3 CH, skip first tr, 1 TR in each tr, ending 1 TR in 3rd of 3 ch, turn.

Row 3: 3 CH, skip first tr, *1 TR CR over next 3 tr, 1 TR in each of following 3 tr, repeat from *, ending 1 TR CR over last 3 tr, 1 TR in 3rd of 3 ch, turn.

Row 4: As row 2.

Row 5: 3 CH, skip first tr, *1 TR in each of next 3 tr, 1 TR CR over following 3 tr, repeat from *, ending 1 TR in each of last 3 tr, 1 TR in 3rd of 3 ch, turn.

Repeat rows 2–5.

9 Relief Stitches

Relief, or raised, stitches are formed by inserting the hook around the stem of the stitch below. The hook is normally inserted from right to left, either from the front or the back, as shown on page 31. The stitch patterns form firm, close-textured fabrics.

Front raised trebles

Any number of sts (add 2 for foundation ch).

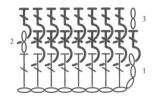

Special stitch – Front raised treble (FRTR) = yrh, insert hook (from the front) around stem of treble below from right to left, then complete treble in the usual way (see page 31).

Row 1: 1 TR in 4th ch from hook, 1 TR in each ch to end, turn.

Row 2: 2 CH, skip first tr, *1 FRTR around next tr, repeat from *, ending 1 FRTR around 3 ch, turn.

Row 3: As row 2, ending 1 FRTR around 2 ch, turn.

Repeat row 3.

Back raised trebles

Any number of sts (add 2 for foundation ch).

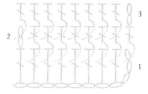

Special stitch – Back raised treble (BRTR) = yrh, insert hook (from the back) around stem of treble below from right to left, then complete treble in the usual way (see page 31).
Row 1: 1 TR in 4th ch from hook, 1 TR in each ch to end, turn.
Row 2: 2 CH, skip first tr, *1 BRTR around next tr, repeat from *, ending 1 BRTR around 3 ch, turn.
Row 3: As row 2, ending 1 BRTR around 2 ch, turn.
Repeat row 3.

Raised treble ridges

Any number of sts (add 2 for foundation ch).

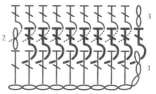

Special stitches – Front raised treble (FRTR); back raised treble (BRTR) as page 31.
Row 1: 1 TR in 4th ch from hook, 1 TR in each ch to end, turn.
Row 2: 2 CH, skip first tr, *1 FRTR around next tr, repeat from *, ending 1 FRTR around 3 ch, turn.
Row 3: 2 CH, skip first tr, *1 BRTR around next tr, repeat from *, ending 1 BRTR around 2 ch, turn.
Row 4: As row 2, ending 1 FRTR around 2 ch, turn.
Repeat rows 3 and 4.

STITCH KEY

◯
chain

treble

Special Stitches

front raised treble
(page 31)

back raised treble
(page 31)

Relief Stitches

Raised treble rib

Even number of sts (add 2 for foundation ch).

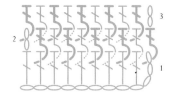

Special stitches – Front raised treble (FRTR); back raised treble (BRTR) as page 31.

Row 1: 1 TR in 4th ch from hook, 1 TR in each ch to end, turn.

Row 2: 2 CH, skip first tr, *1 FRTR around next tr, 1 BRTR around following tr, repeat from *, ending 1 FRTR around 3 ch, turn.

Row 3: As row 2, ending 1 FRTR around 2 ch, turn.

Repeat row 3.

TIP

(Applies to stitches on pages 162–164.)

You can work these raised stitch patterns using longer stitches. To work in double trebles, simply add 1 extra turning ch at the beginning of each row; for triple trebles, add 2 ch, and so on.

Relief trebles

Odd number of sts (add 2 for foundation ch).

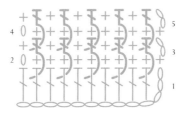

Special stitch – Front raised treble (FRTR) as page 31.

Row 1: 1 TR in 4th ch from hook, 1 TR in each ch to end, turn.

Row 2: 1 CH, skip first tr, 1 DC in each tr, ending 1 DC in 3rd of 3 ch, turn.

Row 3: 2 CH, skip first dc, *1 FRTR around tr below next dc, skip this dc, 1 DC in next dc, repeat from *, ending 1 DC in 1 ch, turn.

Row 4: 1 CH, skip first dc, *1 DC in frtr, 1 DC in dc, repeat from *, ending 1 DC in last frtr, 1 DC in 2nd of 2 ch, turn.

Row 5: 2 CH, skip first dc, 1 FRTR around frtr below next dc, skip this dc, 1 DC in next dc, repeat from *, ending 1 DC in 1 ch, turn.

Repeat rows 4 and 5.

STITCH KEY

o
chain

+
double crochet

treble

Special Stitches

front raised treble (page 31)

back raised treble (page 31)

Relief Stitches

Basketweave stitch

A multiple of 6 sts + 5 (add 2 for foundation ch).

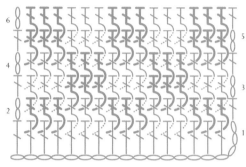

Special stitches – Front raised treble (FRTR); back raised treble (BRTR) as page 31.

Row 1: 1 TR in 4th ch from hook, 1 TR in each ch to end, turn.

Row 2: 2 CH, skip first tr, *1 FRTR around each of next 3 tr, 1 BRTR around each of following 3 tr, repeat from *, ending 1 FRTR around each of last 3 tr, 1 TR in 3rd of 3 ch, turn.

Row 3: 2 CH, skip first tr, *1 BRTR around each of 3 frtr, 1 FRTR around each of 3 brtr, repeat from *, ending 1 BRTR around each of last 3 frtr, 1 TR in 2nd of 2 ch, turn.

Row 4: 2 CH, skip first tr, *1 BRTR around each of 3 brtr, 1 FRTR around each of 3 frtr, repeat from *, ending 1 BRTR around each of last 3 brtr, 1 TR in 2nd of 2 ch, turn.

Row 5: 2 CH, skip first tr, *1 FRTR around each of 3 brtr, 1 BRTR around each of 3 frtr, repeat from *, ending 1 FRTR around each of last 3 brtr, 1 TR in 2nd of 2 ch, turn.

Row 6: 2 CH, skip first tr, *1 FRTR around each of 3 frtr, 1 BRTR around each of 3 brtr, repeat from *, ending 1 FRTR around each of last 3 frtr, 1 TR in 2nd of 2 ch, turn.

Repeat rows 3–6.

Diagonal raised trebles

A multiple of 4 sts + 2 (add 2 for foundation ch).

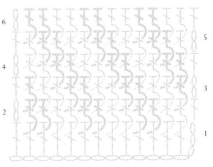

Special stitches – Front raised treble (FRTR); back raised treble (BRTR) as page 31.

Row 1: 1 TR in 4th ch from hook, 1 TR in each ch to end, turn.

Row 2: 2 CH, skip first tr, *1 FRTR around each of next 2 sts, 1 BRTR around each of following 2 sts, repeat from *, ending 1 TR in 3rd of 3 ch, turn.

Row 3: 2 CH, skip first tr, 1 FRTR around first brtr, *1 BRTR around each of next 2 sts, 1 FRTR around each of following 2 sts, repeat from *, ending 1 FRTR around last frtr, 1 TR in 2nd of 2 ch, turn.

Row 4: 2 CH, skip first tr, *1 BRTR around each of next 2 sts, 1 FRTR around each of following 2 sts, repeat from *, ending 1 TR in 2nd of 2 ch, turn.

Row 5: 2 CH, skip first tr, 1 BRTR around first frtr, *1 FRTR around each of next 2 sts, 1 BRTR around each of 2 following sts, repeat from *, ending 1 BRTR around last brtr, 1 TR in 2nd of 2 ch, turn.

Row 6: As row 2, ending 1 TR in 2nd of 2 ch, turn.

Repeat rows 3–6.

STITCH KEY

○
chain

┬
treble

Special Stitches

ʃ
front raised treble
(page 31)

ʃ
back raised treble
(page 31)

Relief wave stitch

A multiple of 6 sts + 3 (add 2 for foundation ch).

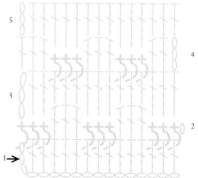

Special stitch – Front raised double crochet (FRDC) = insert hook (from the front) around stem of treble indicated from right to left (in the same way as for front raised treble, page 31), and work a double crochet in the usual way.

Row 1 (wrong side row): 1 TR in 4th ch from hook, 1 TR in each ch to end, turn.

Row 2: 1 CH, 1 FRDC around each of first 3 tr, *1 TR in each of next 3 tr, 1 FRDC around each of following 3 tr, repeat from * to end, turn.

Row 3: 3 CH, skip first frdc, 1 TR in each of next 2 frdc, *1 TR in each of 3 tr, 1 TR in each of 3 frdc, repeat from * to end, turn.

Row 4: 3 CH, skip first tr, 1 TR in each of next 2 tr, *1 FRDC around each of next 3 tr, 1 TR in each of 3 following tr, repeat from *, working last TR in 3rd of 3 ch, turn.

Row 5: 3 CH, skip first tr, 1 TR in each of next 2 tr, *1 TR in each of 3 frdc, 1 TR in each of 3 tr, repeat from *, working last TR in 3rd of 3 ch, turn.

Repeat rows 2–5.

Raised ripple stitch

Odd number of sts (add 2 for foundation ch).

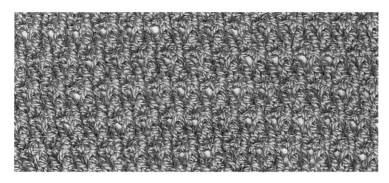

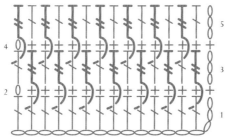

Special stitch – Front raised double treble (FRDTR) = yrh twice, insert hook (from the front) around stem of treble indicated from right to left (see page 31), then complete the double treble in the usual way.

Row 1: 1 TR in 4th ch from hook, 1 TR in each ch to end, turn.

Row 2: 1 CH, skip first st, 1 DC in each st, ending 1 DC in 3rd of 3 ch, turn.

Row 3: 3 CH, skip first dc, *1 FRDTR around tr below next dc, skip this dc, 1 TR in next dc, repeat from *, ending 1 TR in 1 ch, turn.

Row 4: As row 2.

Row 5: 3 CH, skip first dc, *1 TR in next dc, 1 FRDTR around tr below next dc, repeat from *, ending 1 FRDTR around tr below 1 ch, turn.

Repeat rows 2–5.

Raised brick stitch

A multiple of 4 sts + 3 (add 2 for foundation ch).

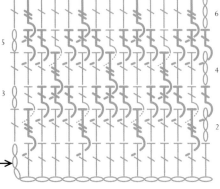

Special stitches – Front raised double treble (FRDTR) = yrh twice, insert hook (from the front) around stem of stitch indicated from right to left (see page 31), then complete the double treble in the usual way; front raised treble (FRTR) and back raised treble (BRTR).

Row 1 (wrong side row): 1 TR in 4th ch from hook, 1 TR in each ch to end, turn.

Row 2: 3 CH, skip first tr, *1 FRDTR around next tr, 1 TR in each of next 3 tr, repeat from *, ending 1 FRDTR around last tr, 1 TR in 3rd of 3 ch, turn.

Row 3: 2 CH, skip first tr, *1 BRTR around frdtr, 1 FRTR around each of 3 tr, repeat from *, ending 1 BRTR around last frdtr, 1 FRTR around 3 ch, turn.

Row 4: 3 CH, skip first frtr, 1 TR in each of next 2 sts, *1 FRDTR around next frtr (the centre 1 of 3), 1 TR in each of next 3 sts, repeat from *, working last TR in 2nd of 2 ch, turn.

Row 5: 2 CH, skip first tr, 1 FRTR around each of next 2 tr, *1 BRTR around frdtr, 1 FRTR around each of 3 tr, repeat from *, working last FRTR around 3 ch, turn.

Row 6: 3 CH, skip first frtr, *1 FRDTR around next frtr (the centre 1 of 3), 1 TR in each of next 3 sts, repeat from *, ending 1 FRDTR around last frtr, 1 TR in 2nd of 2 ch, turn.

Repeat rows 3–6.

Tunisian Stitches

Tunisian is a special type of crochet, worked back and forth without turning the work. On each forward row, a series of loops is made and kept on the hook, then on each return row each stitch is completed in turn. A special Tunisian hook is required: long, with a straight shaft and a knob at the end to prevent the loops from slipping off.

Details of the technique and basic stitches are given on pages 40–41.

STITCH KEY

○
chain

┬
treble

⊤
Tunisian simple stitch (pages 40–41)

Special Stitches

ʓ
front raised treble (page 31)

ʓ
back raised treble (page 31)

front raised double treble

Tunisian simple stitch

Any number of sts (begin with same number of ch).

Row 1: 1 TSS in 2nd ch from hook (first ch = first st), 1 TSS in each ch to end, do not turn.
Row 2: 1 CH (to complete 1 TSS), *yrh, pull through first 2 loops on hook, repeat from * to end – 1 loop remaining on hook, do not turn.
Row 3: Skip first st, 1 TSS in each tss to end, do not turn.
Row 4: As row 2.
Repeat rows 3 and 4.

Tunisian knit stitch

Any number of sts (begin with same number of ch).

Row 1: 1 TSS in 2nd ch from hook (first ch = first st), 1 TSS in each ch to end, do not turn.

Row 2: 1 CH (to complete 1 TSS), *yrh, pull through first 2 loops on hook, repeat from * to end – 1 loop remaining on hook, do not turn.

Row 3: Skip first st, 1 TKS in each st to end, do not turn.

Row 4: 1 CH, *yrh, pull through first 2 loops on hook, repeat from * to end – 1 loop remaining on hook, do not turn.

Repeat rows 3 and 4.

Tunisian purl stitch

Any number of sts (begin with same number of ch).

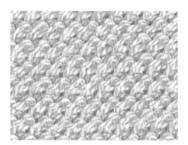

Row 1: 1 TSS in 2nd ch from hook (first ch = first st), 1 TSS in each ch to end, do not turn.

Row 2: 1 CH (to complete 1 TSS), *yrh, pull through first 2 loops on hook, repeat from * to end – 1 loop remaining on hook, do not turn.

Row 3: Skip first st, 1 TPS in each st to end, do not turn.

Row 4: 1 CH, *yrh, pull through first 2 loops on hook, repeat from * to end – 1 loop remaining on hook, do not turn.

Repeat rows 3 and 4.

Tunisian rib

A multiple of 4 sts + 2 (begin with same number of ch).

Row 1: 1 TSS in 2nd ch from hook (first ch = first st), 1 TSS in each ch to end, do not turn.

Row 2: 1 CH (to complete 1 TSS), *yrh, pull through first 2 loops on hook, repeat from * to end – 1 loop remaining on hook, do not turn.

Row 3: Skip first st, 1 TKS in next st, *1 TPS in each of next 2 sts, 1 TKS in each of following 2 sts, repeat from * to end, do not turn.

Row 4: 1 CH, *yrh, pull through first 2 loops on hook, repeat from * to end – 1 loop remaining on hook, do not turn. Repeat rows 3 and 4.

TIP

Use other combinations of knit and purl stitches to make different rib patterns: knit 1, purl 1; knit 3, purl 1; knit 1, purl 2, etc.

STITCH KEY

Tunisian simple stitch (pages 40–41)

Tunisian knit stitch (page 41)

Tunisian purl stitch (page 41)

10

Tunisian bobble stitch

A multiple of 4 sts (begin with same number of ch).

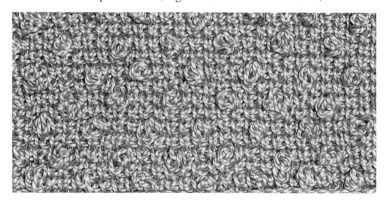

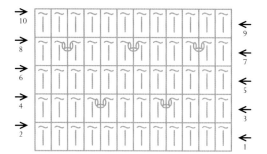

Row 1: 1 TSS in 2nd ch from hook (first ch = first st), 1 TSS in each ch to end, do not turn.

Row 2: 1 CH (to complete 1 TSS), *yrh, pull through first 2 loops on hook, repeat from * to end – 1 loop remaining on hook, do not turn.

Row 3: Skip first st, 1 TSS in each st to end, do not turn.

Row 4: 1 CH, [yrh, pull through first 2 loops on hook] 3 times, *3 CH, [yrh, pull through first 2 loops on hook] 4 times, repeat from * to end – 1 loop remaining on hook, do not turn.

Row 5: As row 3, pushing ch loops to front of work.

Row 6: As row 2.

Row 7: As row 3.

Row 8: 1 CH, yrh, pull through first 2 loops on hook, *3 CH, [yrh, pull through first 2 loops on hook] 4 times, repeat from * until 3 loops remain on hook, 3 CH, [yrh, pull through first 2 loops on hook] twice – 1 loop remaining on hook, do not turn.
Row 9: As row 3, pushing ch loops to front of work.
Row 10: As row 6.
Repeat rows 3–10.

Tunisian honeycomb

Odd number of sts (begin with same number of ch).

Row 1: 1 TSS in 2nd ch from hook (first ch = first st), 1 TSS in each ch to end, do not turn.
Row 2: 1 CH (to complete 1 TSS), *yrh, pull through first 2 loops on hook, repeat from * to end – 1 loop remaining on hook, do not turn.
Row 3: Skip first st, *1 TPS in next st, 1 TSS in following st, repeat from * to end, do not turn.

Row 4: 1 CH, *yrh, pull through first 2 loops on hook, repeat from * to end – 1 loop remaining on hook, do not turn.
Row 5: Skip first st, *1 TSS in next st, 1 TPS in following st, repeat from * to end, do not turn.
Row 6: As row 4.
Repeat rows 3–6.

Tunisian openwork stitch

Even number of sts (begin with same number of chain).

Special stitches – Tunisian 2 together (T2TOG) = insert hook into next st in same way as for TSS, then into following st in the same way, yrh, pull loop through (complete stitch in usual way on return row); Tunisian between stitch (TBS) = insert hook between 2 sts of row below, through to the back, yrh, pull loop through (complete stitch in usual way on return row).

Row 1: 1 TSS in 2nd ch from hook (first ch = first st), 1 TSS in each ch to end, do not turn.

Row 2: 1 CH (to complete 1 TSS), *yrh, pull through first 2 loops on hook, repeat from * to end – 1 loop remaining on hook, do not turn.

Row 3: Skip first st, *T2TOG, inserting hook in next 2 sts, skip 1 st, 1 TBS in sp before next st, repeat from * to last st, 1 TSS in last st, do not turn.

Row 4: 1 CH, *yrh, pull through first 2 loops on hook, repeat from * to end – 1 loop remaining on hook, do not turn. Repeat rows 3 and 4.

Tunisian crossed stitch

Even number of sts (begin with same number of ch).

Row 1: 1 TSS in 2nd ch from hook (first ch = first st), 1 TSS in each ch to end, do not turn.

Row 2: 1 CH (to complete 1 TSS), *yrh, pull through first 2 loops on hook, repeat from * to end – 1 loop remaining on hook, do not turn.

Row 3: Skip first st, *skip next st, 1 TSS in following stitch, 1 TSS in skipped st, repeat from * to last st, 1 TSS in last st, do not turn.

Row 4: 1 CH, *yrh, pull through first 2 loops on hook, repeat from * to end – 1 loop remaining on hook, do not turn. Repeat rows 3 and 4.

Tunisian simple stitch (pages 40–41)

cross 2 Tunisian simple stitches as given

Special Stitches

Tunisian between stitch

Tunisian 2 together on forward row

Tunisian basketweave

A multiple of 6 sts + 5 (begin with same number of ch).

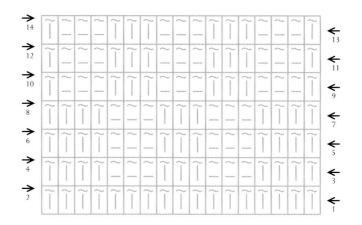

Row 1: 1 TSS in 2nd ch from hook (first ch = first st), 1 TSS in each ch to end, do not turn.

Row 2: 1 CH (to complete 1 TSS), *yrh, pull through first 2 loops on hook, repeat from * to end – 1 loop remaining on hook, do not turn.

Row 3: Skip first st, 1 TSS in each of next 3 sts, *1 TPS in each of next 3 sts, 1 TSS in each of following 3 sts, repeat from * to last st, 1 TSS in last st, do not turn.

Row 4: 1 CH, *yrh, pull through first 2 loops on hook, repeat from * to end – 1 loop remaining on hook, do not turn.

Rows 5–8: Repeat rows 3 and 4 twice more.

Row 9: Skip first st, 1 TPS in each of next 3 sts, *1 TSS in each of next 3 sts, 1 TPS in each of following 3 sts, repeat from * to last st, 1 TSS in last st, do not turn.

Row 10: As row 4.

Rows 11–14: Repeat rows 9 and 10 twice more.

Repeat rows 3–14.

Tunisian lace stitch

A multiple of 4 sts + 1 (begin with same number of ch).

Row 1: 1 TSS in 2nd ch from hook, (first ch = first st), 1 TSS in each ch to end, do not turn.

Row 2: 1 CH (to complete 1 TSS), 2 CH, *yrh, pull through first 5 loops on hook, 1 CH to close the cluster, 3 CH, repeat from *, ending 1 CH to close last cluster – 1 loop remaining on hook, do not turn.

Row 3: Skip first st, *1 TSS in top of first cluster, 1 TSS in each of 3 ch, skip next ch, repeat from * to end.

Row 4: As row 2.

Repeat rows 3 and 4.

11 | *Multi-colour Patterns*

Many interesting effects may be obtained by working stitch patterns in stripes of various kinds, using either boldly contrasting colours or close tones. For the neatest finish when changing colours, use the new colour to work the final "yrh, pull through" of the previous row, as shown on page 23.

Single contrast stripe

Any number of sts (add 2 for foundation ch).

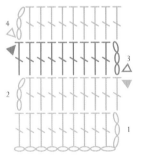

Worked in 2 colours, A and B. For neat edges, change to new colour at end of row by method shown on page 23.

Row 1: Using A, 1 TR in 4th ch from hook, 1 TR in each ch to end, turn.

Work rows in A as required, less one row.

Row 2 (last row of A): 3 CH, skip first tr, 1 TR in each tr, ending 1 TR in 3rd of 3 ch, changing to B, turn. Cut A.

Row 3: Using B, work as previous row changing to A at end in same way. Cut B. Continue in A as required.

Two-row stripes

Any number of sts (add 2 for foundation ch).

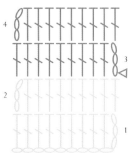

Worked in 2 colours, A and B. For neat edges, change to new colour at end of row by method shown on page 23.

Row 1: 1 TR in 4th ch from hook, 1 TR in each ch to end, turn.

Row 2: 3 CH, skip first tr, 1 TR in each tr, ending 1 TR in 3rd of 3 ch, changing to B, turn. Do not cut A.

Row 3: Using B, 3 CH, skip first tr, 1 TR in each tr, ending 1 TR in 3rd of 3 ch, turn.

Row 4: As row 2, changing to A at end of row in same way, carrying A loosely up the side edge of the work. Do not cut B. Continue in trebles, changing colours every 2 rows without cutting yarns.

TIPS

The stripe patterns on pages 180–183 are all shown in trebles. You can work stripes in other stitches, making neat edges in a corresponding way. At the end of any row, change to the new colour for the final "yrh, pull through", as page 23.

STITCH KEY

⚬
chain

⊤
treble

▼
fasten off

▽
join in

Two-colour, one-row stripes

Any number of sts (add 2 for foundation ch).

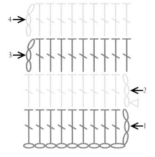

Worked in 2 colours, A and B; a stitch holder (see page 14) is required.

Row 1: Using A, 1 TR in 4th ch from hook, 1 TR in each ch to end, slip loop from hook onto holder, do not turn.

Row 2: Return to beginning of previous row, join B to 3rd of 3 ch, 3 CH, 1 TR in each tr to last tr, yrh, insert hook in last tr and also through loop on holder, yrh, pull through a loop, yrh, pull through first 2 loops on hook, leave B aside and pick up A, yrh, pull through both loops on hook, turn. Do not cut A. Remove holder.

Row 3: Using A, 3 CH, skip first tr, 1 TR in each tr to end, slip loop from hook onto holder, do not turn.

Repeat rows 2 and 3.

Three-colour, one-row stripes

Any number of sts (add 2 for foundation ch).

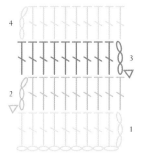

Worked in 3 colours, A, B and C. For neat edges, change to new colour at end of row by method shown on page 23.

Row 1: Using A, 1 TR in 4th ch from hook, 1 TR in each ch to end, changing to B on last tr, turn. Do not cut A.

Row 2: Using B, 3 CH, skip first tr, 1 TR in each tr, ending 1 TR in 3rd of 3 ch, changing to C, turn. Do not cut B.

Row 3: Using C, work as row 2, changing to A at end of row, carrying A loosely up side of work, turn.

Continue in this way changing to the new colour at the end of every row.

Two-colour wave stitch

A multiple of 8 sts + 1.

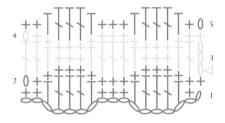

Worked in 2 colours, A and B. For neat edges, change to new colour at end of row by method shown on page 23.

Row 1: Using A, 1 DC in 2nd ch from hook, *1 HTR in next ch, 1 TR in each of next 3 ch, 1 HTR in next ch, 1 DC in each of next 3 ch, repeat from *, ending 1 DC in each of last 2 ch, turn.

Row 2: 1 CH, skip first dc, 1 DC in next dc, *1 DC in htr, 1 DC in each of 3 tr, 1 DC in htr, 1 DC in each of 3 dc, repeat from *, ending 1 DC in last dc, 1 DC in 1 ch, changing to B, turn. Do not cut B.

Row 3: Using B, 3 CH, skip first dc, 1 TR in next dc, *1 HTR in next dc, 1 DC in each of next 3 dc, 1 HTR in next dc, 1 TR in each of next 3 dc, repeat from *, ending 1 TR in last dc, 1 TR in 1 ch, turn.

Row 4: 1 CH, skip first tr, 1 DC in next tr, *1 DC in htr, 1 DC in each of 3 dc, 1 DC in htr, 1 DC in each of 3 tr, repeat from *, ending 1 DC in last tr, 1 DC in 3rd of 3 ch, changing to A, carrying A loosely up side edge of work, turn. Do not cut B.

Row 5: Using A, 1 CH, skip first dc, 1 DC in next dc, *1 HTR in next dc, 1 TR in each of next 3 dc, 1 HTR in next dc, 1 DC in each of next 3 dc, repeat from *, ending 1 DC in last dc, 1 DC in 1 ch, turn. Repeat rows 2–5.

Chevron stripes

A multiple of 8 sts + 1 (add 3 for foundation ch).

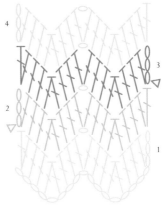

Worked in 3 colours, A, B and C. For neat edges, change to new colour at end of row by method shown on page 23.

Row 1: Using A, 1 TR in 4th ch from hook, *1 TR in each of next 2 ch, 2 TR TOG over next and following alternate ch (leaving 1 ch unworked), 1 TR in each of next 2 ch, [1 TR, 1 CH, 1 TR] in next ch, repeat from *, ending 2 TR in last ch, changing to B, turn. Do not cut A.

Row 2: Using B, 3 CH, 1 TR in first tr, *1 TR in each of next 2 tr, 2 TR TOG over next and

following alternate st (leaving 2 tr tog unworked), 1 TR in each of next 2 tr, [1 TR, 1 CH, 1 TR] in 1 ch sp, repeat from *, ending 2 TR in 3rd of 3 ch, changing to C, turn. Do not cut B.

Row 3: Using C, work as row 2, changing to A at end, carrying A loosely up side of work. Do not cut C.

Row 4: Using A, work as row 2, changing to B at end, carrying B loosely up side edge of work. Do not cut A.

Repeat rows 2–4.

STITCH KEY

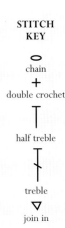

○
chain

+
double crochet

T
half treble

T
treble

▽
join in

Bamboo stitch

A multiple of 4 sts + 2 (add 2 for foundation ch).

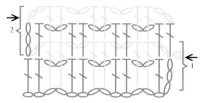

Worked in 2 colours, A and B. A stitch holder (page 14) is required.

Row 1: Using A, 1 TR in 4th ch from hook, *2 CH, skip 2 ch, 1 TR in each of next 2 ch, repeat from * to end, slip loop from hook onto holder, do not turn. Return to beginning of row, join B to 3rd of 3 ch, 2 CH, skip next tr, *1 TR in each of 2 empty foundation ch below, (enclosing 2 ch in A), 2 CH, skip 2 tr in A, repeat from *, ending 2 CH, skip 1 tr in A, pull loop of A from holder through loop on hook, turn. Remove holder.

Row 2: Using A, 3 CH, skip first tr in A below, 1 TR in next tr in A below (enclosing 1 ch in B), *2 CH, skip 2 tr in B, 1 TR in each of 2 tr in A below (enclosing 2 ch in B), repeat from *, ending 1 TR in 3rd of 3 ch in A below, slip loop from hook onto holder, do not turn. Return to beginning of row, using B, 1 SS in 3rd of 3 ch in A, 2 CH, skip next tr, *1 TR in each of 2 tr in B below (enclosing 2 ch in A), 2 CH, skip 2 tr in A, repeat from *, ending 2 CH, skip 1 tr in A, pull loop of A from holder through loop on hook, turn. Remove holder.

Repeat row 2.

Two-colour checkers

A multiple of 8 sts + 4 (add 2 for foundation ch).

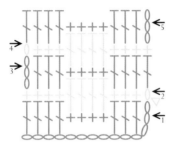

Worked in 2 colours, A and B. A stitch holder (page 14) is required.

Row 1: Using A, 1 TR in 4th ch from hook, 1 TR in each of next 2 ch, *1 DC in each of next 4 ch, 1 TR in each of following 4 ch, repeat from * to end, slip loop from hook onto holder, do not turn. Do not cut A.

Row 2: Return to beginning of previous row, join B to 3rd of 3 ch, 1 CH, 1 DC in each of 3 tr, *1 TR in each of 4 dc, 1 DC in each of 4 tr, repeat from *, working last "pull through" of final dc with loop of A from holder, turn. Do not cut B. Remove holder.

Row 3: Using A, 3 CH, skip first dc, 1 TR in each of next 3 dc, *1 DC in each of 4 tr, 1 TR in each of 4 dc, repeat from *, working last TR in 1 ch, slip loop from hook onto holder, do not turn. Do not cut A. Repeat rows 2 and 3, as required, ending with row 3.

MULTI-COLOUR PATTERNS

Three-colour block stitch

A multiple of 6 sts + 3 (add 3 for foundation ch).

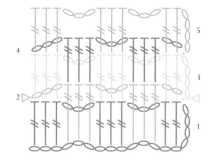

Worked in 3 colours, A, B and C. For neat edges, change to new colour at end of row by method shown on page 23.
Row 1: Using A, 1 DTR in 5th ch from hook, 1 DTR in next ch, *3 CH, skip 3 ch, 1 DTR in each of next 3 ch, repeat from

* changing to B at end of row, turn. Do not cut A.
Row 2: Using B, 3 CH, skip first 3 dtr, *1 DTR in each of 3 empty foundation ch below (enclosing 3 ch in A), 3 CH, skip 3 dtr, repeat from *, ending 2 CH, skip 2 dtr, change to C, 1 SS in 3rd of 3 ch in A, turn. Do not cut B.
Row 3: Using C, 4 CH, skip 1 ss, 1 DTR in each of 2 dtr in A below (enclosing 2 ch in B), *3 CH, skip 3 dtr in B, 1 DTR in each of 3 dtr in A below (enclosing 3 ch in B), repeat from * to end, changing to A at end of row, turn. Do not cut C.
Row 4: Using A, as row 2, changing to B at end.
Row 5: Using B, as row 3, changing to C at end.
Continue in this way, repeating rows 2 and 3, changing to next colour at end of every row.

Two-colour relief rib

A multiple of 3 sts + 2.

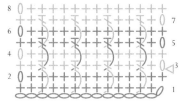

Worked in 2 colours, A and B. For neat edges, change to new colour at end of row by method shown on page 23.

Special stitch: Front raised treble (FRTR) as page 31.

Row 1: Using A, 1 DC in 2nd ch from hook, 1 DC in each ch to end, turn.

Row 2: 1 CH, skip first dc, 1 DC in each st ending 1 DC in 1 ch, changing to B, turn. Do not cut A.

Row 3: Using B, 1 CH, skip first dc, 1 DC in next dc, *1 FRTR around st below next dc, (skip this dc), 1 DC in each of next 2 dc, repeat from *, working last DC in 1 ch, turn.

Row 4: Using B, as row 2, changing to A.

Row 5: Using A, as row 3.

Row 6: Using A, as row 4, changing to B at end. Repeat rows 3–6.

STITCH KEY

○
chain

•
slip stitch

+
double crochet

double treble

▽
join in new yarn

Special Stitch

front raised treble
(page 31)

Two-colour brick stitch

A multiple of 4 sts + 1.

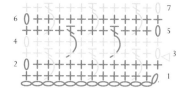

Worked in 2 colours, A and B. For neat edges, change to new colour at end of row by method shown on page 23.

Special stitch: Front raised treble (FRTR) as page 31.

Row 1: Using A, 1 DC in 2nd ch from hook, 1 DC in each ch to end, turn.

Row 2: 1 CH, skip first dc, 1 DC in each st ending 1 DC in 1 ch, changing to B, turn. Do not cut A.

Row 3: Using B, 1 CH, skip first dc, 1 DC in next dc, *1 FRTR around st below next dc (skip this dc), 1 DC in each of next 3 dc, repeat from *, ending 1 DC in last dc, 1 DC in 1 ch, turn.

Row 4: Using B, as row 2, changing to A at end.

Row 5: Using A, 1 CH, skip first dc, *1 DC in each of next 3 dc, 1 FRTR around st below next dc (skip this dc), repeat from * omitting last FRTR and working 1 DC in 1 ch, turn.

Repeat rows 2–5.

Two-colour scale stitch

A multiple of 6 sts + 1 (add 3 for foundation ch).

STITCH KEY

⬭ chain

• slip stitch

+ double crochet

┬ treble

5 trebles together

▽ join in new yarn

← direction of working

Special Stitch

front raised treble

Worked in 2 colours, A and B. A stitch holder (as page 14) is required.

Row 1: Using A, 2 TR in 4th ch from hook, *skip 2 ch, 1 DC in next ch, skip 2 ch, 5 TR in next ch, repeat from *, ending 3 TR in last ch, slip loop from hook onto holder, do not turn.

Row 2: Return to beginning of previous row, join B to 3rd of 3 ch, 3 CH, *5 TR TOG over [2 tr, 1 dc, 2 tr], 2 CH, 1 DC in next tr (the centre tr of 5), 2 CH, repeat from *, ending 1 DC in 3rd of 3 tr, working last "pull through" of this dc with loop of A from holder, turn. Do not cut B.

Row 3: Using A, 3 CH, 2 TR in first dc, *skip 2 ch, 1 DC in 5 tr tog, skip 2 ch, 5 TR in next dc, repeat from *, ending 3 TR in first of 3 ch, slip loop from hook onto holder, do not turn.

Row 4: As row 2.
Repeat rows 3 and 4.

Three-colour fan stitch

A multiple of 6 sts + 1.

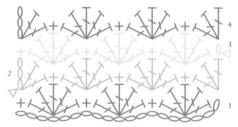

Worked in 3 colors, A, B and C. For neat edges, change to new colour at end of row by method shown on page 23.

Row 1: Using A, 5 TR in 4th ch from hook, *skip 2 ch, 1 DC in next ch, skip 2 ch, 5 TR in next ch, repeat from * ending 1 DC in last ch, changing to B, turn. Do not cut A.

Row 2: Using B, 3 CH, 2 TR in first dc, *skip 2 tr, 1 DC in next tr (the centre tr of 5), skip 2 tr, 5 TR in next dc, repeat from * ending 3 TR in 1 ch, changing to C, turn. Do not cut B.

Row 3: Using C, 1 CH, skip first 3 tr, *5 TR in next dc, skip 2 tr, 1 DC in next tr (the centre tr of 5), skip 2 tr, repeat from * ending 1 DC in 3rd of 3 ch, changing to A, turn. Do not cut C.

Repeat rows 2 and 3, changing to next colour at end of every row.

Birdsfoot spikes

A multiple of 6 sts + 1.

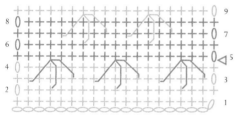

Worked in 2 colours, A and B. For neat edges, change to new colour at end of row by method shown on page 23.

Special stitch – Spike cluster (SCL) = insert hook to right of dc 1 row below and 2 sts to right of next dc, yrh, pull loop through, insert hook to right of dc 2 rows below next dc, yrh, pull loop through, insert hook to right of dc 1 row below and 2 sts to left, (lengthen all these loops so the work lies flat), yrh, pull through 4 loops on hook.

Row 1: Using A, 1 DC in 2nd ch from hook, 1 DC in each ch to end, turn.

Row 2: 1 CH, skip first dc, 1 DC in each st ending 1 DC in 1 ch, turn.

Row 3: As row 2.

Row 4: As row 2, changing to B at end. Do not cut A.

Row 5: 1 CH, skip first dc, 1 DC in each of next 2 dc, *1 SCL in place of next dc, 1 DC in each of next 5 dc, repeat from * ending 1 DC in each of last 2 dc, 1 DC in 1 ch, turn.

Rows 6 and 7: As row 2.

Row 8: As row 2, changing to A at end. Do not cut B.

Row 9: 1 CH, skip first dc, *1 DC in each of next 5 dc, 1 SCL in place of next dc, repeat from * ending 1 DC in each of last 5 dc, 1 DC in 1 ch, turn.

Repeat rows 2–9.

STITCH KEY

o
chain

+
double crochet

T
treble

▽
join in new yarn

Special Stitch

spike cluster

Multi-colour Patterns

193

Eyelash stitch

A multiple of 6 sts + 3.

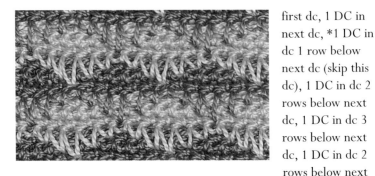

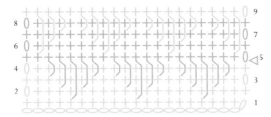

Worked in 2 colours, A and B.
For neat edges, change to new
colour at end of row by method
shown on page 23.

Row 1: Using A, 1 DC in 2nd
ch from hook, 1 DC in each ch
to end, turn.

Row 2: 1 CH, skip first dc, 1
DC in each st ending 1 DC in 1
ch, turn.

Row 3: As row 2.

Row 4: As row 2, changing to
B at end. Do not cut A.

Row 5: Using B, 1 CH, skip

first dc, 1 DC in
next dc, *1 DC in
dc 1 row below
next dc (skip this
dc), 1 DC in dc 2
rows below next
dc, 1 DC in dc 3
rows below next
dc, 1 DC in dc 2
rows below next
dc, 1 DC in dc 1
row below next
dc, 1 DC in next
dc, repeat from *
to last st, 1 DC in
1 ch, turn.

Rows 6 and 7:
As row 2.

Row 8: As row 2, changing to
A at end. Do not cut B.

Row 9: 1 CH, skip first dc, *1
DC in dc 3 rows below next dc,
1 DC in dc 2 rows below next
dc, 1 DC in dc 1 row below
next dc, 1 DC in next dc, 1 DC
in dc 1 row below next dc, 1
DC in dc 2 rows below next dc,
repeat from * to last 2 sts, 1
DC in dc 3 rows below last dc,
1 DC in 1 ch, turn.
Repeat rows 2–9.

Rake stitch

A multiple of 10 sts + 7.

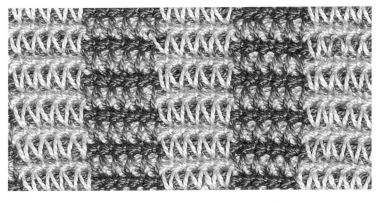

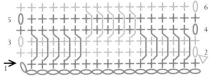

Worked in 2 colours, A and B. For neat edges, change to new colour at end of row by method shown on page 23.

Row 1 (wrong side row): Using A, 1 DC in 2nd ch from hook, 1 DC in each ch, changing to B at end, turn. Do not cut A.

Row 2: Using B, 1 CH, skip first dc, 1 DC in each st ending 1 DC in 1 ch, turn.

Row 3: As row 2, changing to A at end. Do not cut B.

Row 4: Using A, 1 CH, skip first dc, *[1 DC into dc in A, 2 rows below next dc] 5 times, 1 DC in each of next 5 dc, repeat from * ending [1 DC into dc in A, 2 rows below next dc] 5 times, 1 DC in 1 ch, turn.

Row 5: As row 2, changing to B at end. Do not cut A.

Row 6: Using B, 1 CH, skip first dc, *1 DC in each of next 5 dc, [1 DC into dc in B, 2 rows below next dc] 5 times, repeat from * ending 1 DC in each of last 5 dc, 1 DC in 1 ch, turn.

Repeat rows 3–6.

STITCH KEY

◦
chain

+
double crochet

�
double crochet into indicated row below

▽
join in new yarn

Harlequin stitch

A multiple of 8 sts + 1.

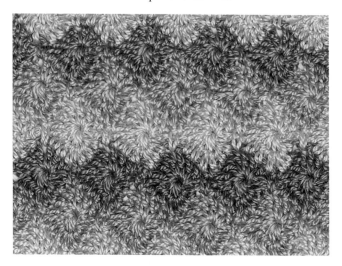

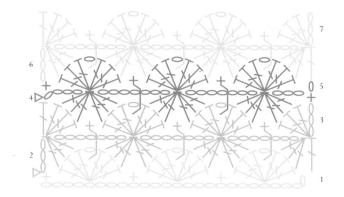

Worked in 3 colours, A, B and C. For neat edges, change to new colour at end of row by method shown on page 23.

Row 1: Using A, [3 TR, 1 CH, 3 TR] in 5th ch from hook, skip 3 ch, 1 DC in next ch, *skip 3 ch, [3 TR, 1 CH, 3 TR] in next ch, skip 3 ch, 1 DC in next ch, repeat from *, changing to B at end, turn. Do not cut A.

Row 2: Using B, 3 CH, skip first dc, 3 TR TOG over next 3 tr, *7 CH, skip 1 ch, 6 TR TOG over next 6 tr (leaving 1 dc between groups unworked), repeat from * ending 3 TR TOG over last 3 tr, 1 TR in 1 ch, turn.

Row 3: 3 CH, skip first tr, 3 TR in top of 3 tr tog, *1 DC in 1 ch sp between trs 1 row below (enclosing centre of 7 ch), [3 TR, 1 CH, 3 TR] in top of 6 tr tog, repeat from * ending 3 TR in top of 3 tr tog, 1 TR in 3rd of 3 ch, changing to C, turn. Do not cut B.

Row 4: Using C, 4 CH, skip first tr, *6 TR TOG over next 6 tr (leaving 1 dc between groups unworked), 7 CH, skip 1 ch, repeat from * ending 3 CH, 1 DC in 3rd of 3 ch, turn.

Row 5: 1 CH, skip [first dc and 3 ch], *[3 TR, 1 CH, 3 TR] in top of 6 tr tog, 1 DC in 1 ch sp between dcs 1 row below (enclosing centre of 7 ch), repeat from *, ending 1 DC in first of 4 ch, changing to A, turn. Do not cut C.

Repeat rows 2–5, changing colours every 2 rows. Carry colours not in use loosely up side edge of work.

STITCH KEY

◯
chain

+
double crochet

T
treble

6 trebles together

double crochet in chain space below

△
join in new yarn

Squares

Squares can be used not just for afghans (throws) but also for cushions, bags and simple garments. They are fun to work, and after making the first two or three, you probably won't need to read the instructions again. Squares may be joined together by several methods, as shown on pages 24, 25 and 28.

Plain ridged square

Colours may be changed at the beginning of any round, (see page 23).

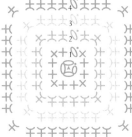

JOINING SQUARES

Plain Ridged Square
Join squares edge to edge with one of the seams on pages 24–25.

Double Square
Join squares edge to edge with one of the seams on page 24–25.

Begin with 4 CH, 1 SS in first ch made.

Round 1: 1 CH, 11 DC into ring, 1 SS in first ch of round.

Round 2: 1 CH, 1 DC in back loop of first dc, 3 DC in back loop of next dc, [1 DC in back loop of each of next 2 dc, 3 DC in back loop of following dc] 3 times, 1 SS in first ch of round.

Round 3: 1 CH, [1 DC in back loop of each dc to corner, 3 DC in back loop of dc at corner (which is the centre dc of 3 worked in same place)] 4 times, 1 SS in first ch of round. Repeat round 3 to size required.

Treble square

Colours may be changed at the beginning of any round.

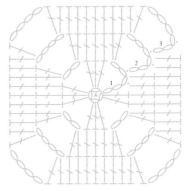

Begin with 4 CH, 1 SS into first ch made.

Round 1: 5 CH, [3 TR into ring, 2 CH] 3 times, 2 TR into ring, 1 SS in 3rd of 5 ch at beginning of round.

Round 2: 1 SS in next ch, 6 CH, 2 TR in first ch sp, *1 TR in each of 3 tr, [2 TR, 4 CH, 2 TR] in ch sp, repeat from * twice more, 1 TR in each of 2 tr, 1 TR in 3rd of 5 ch at beginning previous round, 1 TR in next ch sp, 1 SS in 3rd of 6 ch at beginning this round.

Round 3: 1 SS in next ch, 6 CH, 2 TR in first ch sp, *1 TR in each tr to next corner, [2 TR, 4 CH, 2 TR] in ch sp, repeat from * twice more, 1 TR in each tr along 4th side, 1 TR in 3rd of 6 ch at beginning previous round, 1 TR in next ch sp, 1 SS in 3rd of 6 ch at beginning this round. Repeat round 3 to size required. On each round, 4 extra trebles are worked on each side of the square.

Puff stitch square

Colours may be changed at the beginning of any round.

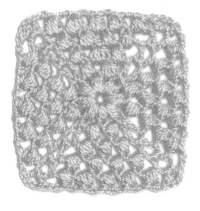

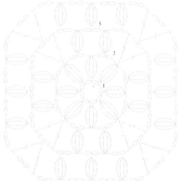

**JOINING
SQUARES**

**Puff Stitch
Square**
Join squares
edge to edge
with one of
the seams on
pages 24–25.

**Old
American
Square**
Join squares
edge to edge
with one of
the seams on
pages 24–25.

Special stitch – Puff stitch
(PS) = [yrh, insert hook as
given, yrh, pull loop through] 4
times in same place, yrh, pull
through 9 loops on hook.
Begin with 8 CH, 1 SS into first
ch made.
Round 1: [1 PS, 2 CH] 8 times
into ring, 1 SS in top of first ps.
Round 2: 1 SS in next ch sp, 1
PS in same ch sp, 2 CH, 1 PS in
next ch sp, 2 CH, *[1 TR, 2 CH,
1 TR] in top of next ps, 2 CH, [1
PS in next ch sp, 2 CH] twice,
repeat from * twice more, [1
TR, 2 CH, 1 TR] in top of last

ps, 2 CH, 1 SS in top of first ps
of round.
Round 3: 1 SS in next ch sp, 1
PS in same ch sp, *2 CH, [1 PS
in next ch sp, 2 CH] in each ch
sp to corner, [1 TR, 2 CH, 1 TR]
in 2 ch sp (between 2 tr), repeat
from * 3 more times, 2 CH, [1
PS in next ch sp, 2 CH] to end
of round, 1 SS in top of first ps
of round.
Repeat round 3 to size required.
On each round, 1 extra Puff
stitch is worked on each side of
the square.

Old American square

This square is normally worked using a new colour for each round.

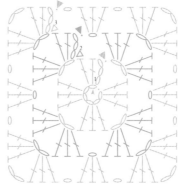

Begin with 6 CH, 1 SS into first ch made.

Round 1: 3 CH, 2 TR into ring, 2 CH, [3 TR into ring, 2 CH] 3 times, 1 SS in 3rd of 3 ch at beginning of round, fasten off.

Round 2: Rejoin yarn to next 2 ch sp, 3 CH, [2 TR, 2 CH, 3 TR] in same ch sp, *1 CH, [3 TR, 2 CH, 3 TR] in next 2 ch sp, 1 CH, repeat from * twice more, 1 SS in 3rd of 3 ch at beginning of round, fasten off.

Round 3: Rejoin yarn to next 2 ch sp, 3 CH, [2 TR, 2 CH, 3 TR] in same ch sp, *1 CH, [3 TR in 1 ch sp, 1 CH] in each 1 ch sp to corner, [3 TR, 2 CH, 3 TR] in 2 ch sp at corner, repeat from * twice more, 1 CH, [3 TR in 1 ch sp, 1 CH] in each 1 ch sp to beginning of round, 1 SS in 3rd of 3 ch at beginning of round, fasten off.

Repeat round 3 to size required. On each round one extra group of 3 trebles is worked on each side of the square.

STITCH KEY

o
chain

.
slip stitch

T
treble

▲
starting point

▲
fasten off

Δ
join in new yarn

Special Stitch

puff stitch

Cross in a square

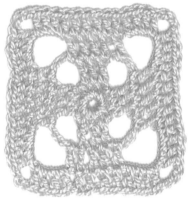 

JOINING
SQUARES

**Cross in a
Square**
Join squares
edge to edge
with one of
the seams on
pages 24–25.

**Daisy in a
Square**
Join squares at
the top of each
3 tr tog on last
round, by
method shown
on page 28.

Begin with 6 CH, 1 SS into first ch made.

Round 1: [3 DC into ring, 1 CH] 4 times, 1 SS in first dc of round.

Round 2: 3 CH, skip first dc, 1 TR in each of next 2 dc, 5 CH, [skip 1 ch, 1 TR in each of next 3 dc, 5 CH] 3 times, 1 SS in 3rd of 3 ch at beginning of round.

Round 3: 3 CH, 1 TR in each of 2 tr, [1 TR, 7 CH, 1 TR] in 5 ch sp, *1 TR in each of 3 tr, [1 TR, 7 CH, 1 TR] in next 5 ch sp, repeat from * twice more, 1 SS in 3rd of 3 ch at beginning of round.

Round 4: 3 CH, 1 TR in each of 3 tr, [4 TR, 2 CH, 4 TR] in 7 ch sp, *1 TR in each of 5 tr, [4 TR, 2 CH, 4 TR] in 7 ch sp, repeat from * twice more, 1 TR in next tr, 1 SS in 3rd of 3 ch at beginning of round, fasten off.

TIP
Try changing to a new colour (as shown on page 23) for round 4.

Daisy in a square

Begin with 5 CH, 1 SS in first ch made.

Round 1: 12 DC into ring, 1 SS in first dc of round.

Round 2: [11 CH, 1 SS in next dc] 12 times.

Round 3: 1 SS in each of first 6 ch of first ch loop, 4 CH, 1 DC in 6th ch of next loop, 4 CH, [3 TR TOG, 4 CH, 3 TR TOG] in next loop, *4 CH, [1 DC in 6th ch of next loop, 4 CH] twice, [3 TR TOG, 4 CH, 3 TR TOG] in next loop, repeat from * twice more, 4 CH, 1 DC in same place as 6th ss at beginning of round.

Round 4: 1 SS in each of next 2 ch, 3 CH, 2 TR TOG in same 4 ch sp, 4 CH, 1 DC in next 4 ch sp, 4 CH, [3 TR TOG, 4 CH, 3 TR TOG] in 4 ch sp at corner, *4 CH, 1 DC in next 4 ch sp, 4 CH, 3 TR TOG in next 4 ch sp, 4 CH, 1 DC in next 4 ch sp, 4 CH, [3 TR TOG, 4 CH, 3 TR TOG] in 4 ch sp at corner, repeat from * twice more, 4 CH, 1 DC in next 4 ch sp, 4 CH, 1 SS in 3rd of 3 ch at beginning of round, fasten off.

Wheel in a square

Worked in 2 colours, A and B.

**JOINING
SQUARES**

**Wheel in a
Square**
Join squares
edge to edge
with one of
the seams on
pages 24–25.

**French
Square**
Join on
subsequent
squares as you
work the last
round, by
linking the
picots (see
page 28).

Using A, begin with 8 CH, 1 SS
in first ch made.
Round 1: 6 CH, [1 TR into
ring, 3 CH] 7 times, 1 SS in 3rd
of 6 ch at beginning of round,
fasten off A.
Round 2: Join B to next ch, 3
CH, 3 TR in same ch sp, 3 CH,
[4 TR in next 3 ch sp, 3 CH] 7
times, 1 SS in 3rd of 3 ch at
beginning of round, fasten off B.
Round 3: Join A to first of last
3 ch worked, 3 CH, 5 TR in
same 3 ch sp, 1 CH, 6 TR in
next 3 ch sp, 3 CH, [6 TR in

next 3 ch sp, 1 CH, 6 TR in next
3 ch sp, 3 CH] 3 times, 1 SS in
3rd of 3 ch at beginning of
round, fasten off A.
Round 4: Join B to next 1 ch
sp, 3 CH, *1 DC between 3rd
and 4th tr of next group, 3 CH,
[2 TR, 3 CH, 2 TR] in next 3 ch
sp, 3 CH, 1 DC between 3rd
and 4th tr of next group, 3 CH,
1 DC in next 1 ch sp, repeat
from * omitting last dc at end of
round, 1 SS in first ch of round,
fasten off.

French square

Special stitches – 5-CH picot = 5 CH, 1 SS in top of st at base of these 5 ch; 3-CH picot = 3 CH, 1 SS in top of st at base of these 3 ch.

Begin with 6 CH, 1 SS in first ch made.

Round 1: 4 CH, [1 TR into ring, 1 CH] 11 times, 1 SS in 3rd of 4 ch at beginning of round.

Round 2: 1 SS in next ch, 2 CH, 3 HTR TOG under same ch, 2 CH, 4 HTR TOG in next 1 ch sp, 3 CH, *1 DTR in next tr, 3 CH, [4 HTR TOG in next 1 ch sp, 2 CH] twice, 4 HTR TOG in next 1 ch sp, 3 CH, repeat from * twice more, 1 DTR in next tr, 3 CH, 4 HTR TOG in next 1 ch sp, 2 CH, 1 SS in top of 3 htr tog at beginning of round.

Round 3: 1 CH, *1 DC in top of group, 5-CH Picot, 2 CH, skip [2 ch, 1 group], 5 TR in next 3 ch sp, 1 CH, 1 DTR in dtr, 3-CH Picot, 1 CH, 5 TR in next 3 ch sp, 2 CH, skip [1 group, 2 ch], repeat from * 3 more times, 1 SS in first dc of round, fasten off.

Sun square

**JOINING
SQUARES**

Sun Square
Join on
subsequent
squares as you
work the last
round, by
linking the
picots (see
page 28).

206

Special stitches – 5-CH Picot = 5 CH, 1 SS in top of st at base of these 5 ch; 3-CH Picot = 3 CH, 1 SS in top of st at base of these 3 ch.

Begin with a finger wrap (page 27).

Round 1: 1 SS into ring, 6 CH, [1 DC into ring, 5 CH] 3 times, 1 SS in first of 6 ch at beginning of round.

Round 2: 1 CH, 7 DC in first 5 ch sp, [1 DC in next dc, 5-CH PICOT, 7 DC in next 5 ch sp] 3 times, 1 SS in 1 ch at beginning of round, 2 CH, 1 TR in same ch as last ss made.

Round 3: *4 CH, skip 1 dc, 1 DTR in each of next 5 dc, skip 1 dc, 4 CH, 1 SS in next picot, repeat from * twice more, 4 CH, skip 1 dc, 1 DTR in each of next 5 dc, skip 1 dc, 1 CH, 1 TR in last picot.

Round 4: 3 CH, work [1 TR under last tr of previous round, 1 DTR in picot of previous round, 2 TR in next 4 ch sp] all TOG, 5 CH, *work [1 DTR in first of 5 DTR, 1 TR in each of next 2 dtr] all TOG, 5 CH, work [1 TR in same dtr as last insertion, 1 TR in next dtr, 1 DTR in next dtr] all TOG, 5 CH, work [2 TR in next 4 ch sp, 1 DTR in picot of previous round, 2 TR in next 4 ch sp] all TOG, 5 CH, repeat from * twice more, work [1 DTR in first of 5 dtr, 1 TR in each of next 2 dtr] all TOG, 5 CH, work [1 TR in same dtr as last insertion, 1 TR in next dtr, 1 DTR in next dtr] all TOG, 5 CH, 1 SS in top of first group at beginning of round.

Round 5: 1 CH, 6DC in first 5 ch sp, *[4 DC, 3-CH PICOT, 3 DC] in 5 ch sp at corner, 6 DC in next 5 ch sp, [1 DC, 3-CH PICOT] in top of next group, 6 DC in next 5 ch sp, repeat from * twice more, [4 DC, 3-CH PICOT, 3 DC] in 5 ch sp at corner, 6 DC in next 5 ch sp, [1 SS, 3-CH PICOT] in 1 ch at beginning of round, fasten off.

Three-colour square

Worked in three colours, A, B and C.

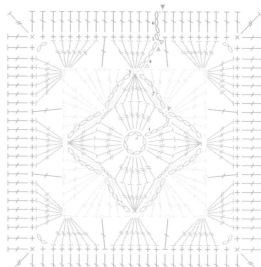

**JOINING
SQUARES**

**Three-colour
Square**
Join squares
edge to edge
with one of the
seams on pages
24–25.

The Stitch Collection

Using A, begin with 8 CH, 1 SS in first ch made.

Round 1: 7 CH, 6 DTR into ring, [3 CH, 6 DTR into ring] 3 times, 1 SS in 4th of 7 ch at beginning of round.

Round 2: 1 SS in each of next 2 ch, [5 CH, 6 DTR TOG over next 6 dtr, 5 CH, 1 SS in 2nd of 3 ch] 4 times, working last SS in same place as 2nd ss at beginning of round, fasten off A.

Round 3: Join B with 1 SS in top of next group, *[3 DTR, 1 CH, 3 DTR, 2 CH, 3 DTR, 1 CH, 3 DTR] all in next 3 ch sp of round 1, 1 SS in top of next group, repeat from * 3 more times, working last SS in same place as first ss of round, fasten off B.

Round 4: Join A to same place, 4 CH, 5 DTR in same ss, *skip [3 dtr, 1 ch, 3 dtr], [6 DTR, 2 CH, 6 DTR] in 2 ch sp at corner, skip [3 DTR, 1 ch, 3 dtr], 6 DTR in next ss, repeat from * twice more, skip [3 dtr, 1 ch, 3 dtr], [6 DTR, 2 CH, 6 DTR] in 2 ch sp at corner, skip [3 dtr, 1 ch, 3 dtr], 1 SS in 4th of 4 ch at beginning of round, fasten off.

Round 5: Join C to same place, 1 CH, 1 DC in each of 5 dtr, *1 TR in 1 ch sp of round 3 below, 1 DC in each of 6 dtr, 3 DC in 2 ch sp at corner, 1 DC in each of 6 dtr, 1 TR in 1 ch sp of round 3 below, 1 DC in each of 6 dtr, repeat from * twice more, 1 TR in 1 ch sp of round 3 below, 1 DC in each of 6 dtr, 3 DC in 2 ch sp at corner, 1 DC in each of 6 dtr, 1 TR in 1 ch sp of round 3 below, 1 SS in 1 ch at beginning of round.

Round 6: 3 CH, *1 TR in each st to centre dc of 3 at corner, 1 DTR in this dc, repeat from * three more times, 1 TR in each of last 7 dc, 1 TR in last tr, 1 SS in 3rd of 3 ch at beginning of round, fasten off C.

STITCH KEY

o
chain

.
slip stitch

+
double crochet

treble

double treble

▲
starting point

▲
fasten off

△
join in new yarn

13 Shapes and Motifs

Geometric shapes (including circles) may be worked in rounds.
Some, such as hexagons and triangles, may be joined together
in the same way as squares (pages 24–25). Shapes with picots
may be joined as shown on page 28. Shaped motifs, such as
flowers, leaves and shells may be used to decorate crochet
articles such as bags, hats and cushions, or stitched onto a
fabric background.

Clover leaf

Begin with 5 CH, 1 SS in first ch made.

Round 1: 1 CH, 10 DC into ring, 1 SS in first ch of round.

Round 2: 1 CH, 1 DC in first dc, *4 CH, 3 DTR TOG, inserting hook in same place as last dc, then in each of next 2 dc, 4 CH, 1 DC in same place as last insertion, 1 DC in next dc, repeat from * twice more, make stalk: 7 CH (or number required), turn, 1 DC in 2nd ch from hook, 1 DC in each ch, 1 SS in first ch of round, fasten off.

Four-petal flower

Worked in 2 colours, A and B.

Using A, begin with 4 CH, 1 SS in first ch made.

Round 1: 1 CH, 7 DC into ring, 1 SS in first ch of this round, fasten off A.

Round 2: Join B to same place, [3 CH, 3 TR TOG all in back loop of next dc, 3 CH, 1 DC into centre ring, skip next dc] 4 times, then make stalk: 1 SS in first of 3 ch at beginning of this round, 10 CH (or any number required), turn, 1 SS in 2nd ch from hook, 1 SS in each ch, fasten off.

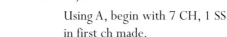

Five-petal flower

Worked in 2 colours, A and B.

Using A, begin with 7 CH, 1 SS in first ch made.

Round 1: 1 CH, 14 DC into ring, 1 SS in first ch of round, fasten off A.

Round 2: Join B to same place, 4 CH, *4 DTR TOG, inserting hook twice in next dc and twice in following dc, 3 CH, 1 DC in next dc, 3 CH, repeat from * 3 more times, 4 DTR TOG, inserting hook as before, 3 CH, 1 SS in first ch of round, fasten off.

SHAPES AND MOTIFS

Six-petal flower

Worked in 2 colours, A and B.

Using A, begin with 4 CH, 1 SS in first ch made.

Round 1: 5 CH, [1 TR into ring, 2 CH] 5 times, 1 SS in 3rd of 5 ch at beginning of round, fasten off A.

Round 2: Join B to same place, 5 CH, *3 TRTR TOG, inserting hook 3 times in same 2 ch sp, 5 CH, 1 DC around stem of next tr, inserting hook from right to left, 4 CH, repeat from * 4 more times, 3 TRTR TOG, inserting hook as before, 5 CH, 1 DC around first 2 ch of round 1, 1 SS in first ch of this round, fasten off.

TIP

After fastening off one colour and joining in the next, work the next few stitches over both yarn ends. After completion, pull gently on the yarn ends to tighten them before trimming them off.

Circle in trebles

Colours may be changed at the beginning of any round, (see page 23).

Begin with 5 CH, 1 SS in first ch made.

Round 1: 3 CH, 15 TR into ring, 1 SS in 3rd of 3 ch at beginning of round. (= 16 tr)

Round 2: 3 CH, 1 TR in ch at base of these 3 ch, 2 TR in every tr, 1 SS in 3rd of 3 ch at beginning of round. (= 32 tr)

Round 3: 3 CH, 2 TR in next tr, [1 TR in next tr, 2 TR in next tr] 15 times, 1 SS in 3rd of 3 ch at beginning of round. (= 48 tr)

Round 4: 3 CH, 2 TR in next tr, [1 TR in each of next 2 tr, 2 TR in next tr] 15 times, 1 TR in next tr, 1 SS in 3rd of 3 ch at beginning of round. (= 64 tr) If required, continue in this way, working 16 extra tr on every round.

Wheel circle

Worked in 2 colours, A and B.

Using A, begin with 4 CH, 1 SS in first ch made.

Round 1: 2 CH, 1 HTR into ring, 1 CH, [2 HTR TOG into ring, 1 CH] 7 times, 1 SS in first htr of round, fasten off A.

Round 2: Join B to any 1 ch sp, 3 CH, 1 TR in same space, 2 CH, [2 TR in next 1 ch sp, 2 CH] 7 times, 1 SS in 3rd of 3 ch at beginning of round, fasten off B.

Round 3: Join A to any 2 ch sp, 3 CH, [1 TR, 1 CH, 2 TR] in same space, 1 CH, *[2 TR, 1 CH, 2 TR] in next 2 ch sp, 1 CH, repeat from * 6 more times, 1 SS in 3rd of 3 ch at beginning of round, fasten off A.

Round 4: Join B to any 1 ch sp, 3 CH, 2 TR in same space, 1 CH, [3 TR in next 1 ch sp, 1 CH] 15 times, 1 SS in 3rd of 3 ch at beginning of round, fasten off.

TIP

This wheel circle may also be worked in four colours, using a different colour for each round.

JOINING SHAPES

Hexagon in Doubles
Join hexagons edge to edge with one of the seams on pages 24–25.

214

Hexagon in trebles

Colours may be changed at the beginning of any round.

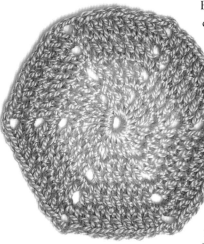

Begin with 4 CH, 1 SS in first ch made.

Round 1: 5 CH, [3 TR into ring, 2 CH] 5 times, 2 TR into ring, 1 SS in 3rd of 5 ch at beginning of round.

Round 2: 1 SS in next ch, 5 CH, 1 TR under next ch, *1 TR in each of 3 tr, [1 TR, 2 CH, 1 TR] in 2 ch sp, repeat from * 4 more times, 1 TR in each of next 3 tr, 1 TR in 3rd of 5 ch at beginning previous round, 1 SS in 3rd of 5 ch at beginning of this round.

Round 3: 1 SS in next ch, 5 CH, 1 TR under next ch, *1 TR in each tr to corner, [1 TR, 2 CH, 1 TR] in 2 ch sp, repeat from * 4 more times, 1 TR in each tr to corner, 1 TR in 3rd of 5 ch at beginning previous round, 1 SS in 3rd of 5 ch at beginning this round.

If required, repeat round 3, working 2 extra tr on each side on every round.

STITCH KEY

○
chain

•
slip stitch

┬
treble

∧
2 half trebles together

◀
fasten off

◁
join in new yarn

▲
starting point

Spiral hexagon

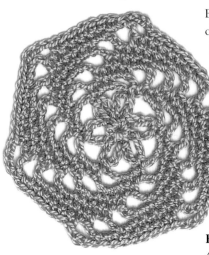

Begin with 4 CH, 1 SS in first ch made.

Round 1: 7 CH, 1 DC into ring, [6 CH, 1 DC into ring] 5 times, 1 SS in first ch of round.

Round 2: 1 SS in each of next 3 ch, [4 CH, 1 DC in next 6 ch loop] 6 times.

Round 3: [4 CH, 2 DC in next 4 ch sp, 1 DC in next dc] 6 times.

Round 4: [4 CH, 2 DC in next 4 ch sp, 1 DC in each of next 2 dc, skip 1 dc] 6 times.

Round 5: [4 CH, 2 DC in next 4 ch sp, 1 DC in each of next 3 dc, skip 1 dc] 6 times.

If required, continue in this way, working 1 extra dc on each side on every round.

JOINING SHAPES

Spiral Hexagon
Join hexagons edge to edge with one of the seams on pages 24–25.

216

Rectangle in trebles

Colours may be changed at the beginning of any round.

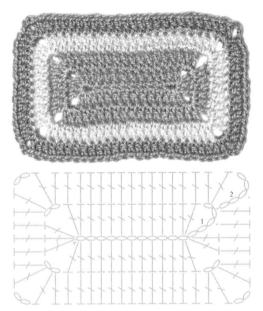

To work a rectangle of any proportions, determine the difference between the final width and length required and calculate the equivalent number of trebles (page 42). Begin with this number of chain + 5. (11 + 5 ch shown on diagram.)

Round 1: 2 TR in 6th ch from hook, 1 TR in each ch to last ch, [2 TR, 2 CH, 3 TR, 2 CH, 2 TR] in last ch, work along lower edge of ch: 1 TR in each ch to ch containing 2 tr, [2 TR, 2 CH, 2 TR] in this ch, 1 SS in 3rd of 5 ch at beginning of round.

Round 2: 1 SS in next ch, 5 CH, 2 TR under next ch, *1 TR in each tr to corner, [2 TR, 2 CH, 2 TR] in 2 ch sp, repeat from * twice more, 1 TR in each tr ending 1 TR in 3rd of 5 ch at beginning of previous round, 1 TR under next ch, 1 SS in 3rd of 5 ch at beginning of this round. If required, continue in this way, working 4 extra tr on each side on every round.

STITCH KEY

◯
chain

•
slip stitch

+
double crochet

T
treble

▲
starting point

Shapes and Motifs

217

Triangle in trebles

Colours may be changed at the beginning of any round.

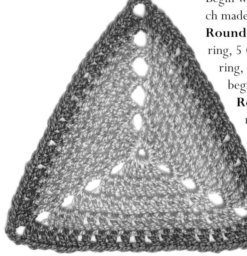

Begin with 6 CH, 1 SS in first ch made.

Round 1: 8 CH, [5 TR into ring, 5 CH] twice, 4 TR into ring, 1 SS in 3rd of 8 ch at beginning of round.

Round 2: 1 SS in each of next 2 ch, 8 CH, 2 TR under next 3 ch, *1 TR in each tr to corner, [2 TR, 5 CH, 2 TR] in 5 ch sp, repeat from * once more, 1 TR in each tr, ending 1 TR in 3rd of 8 ch at beginning previous round, 1 TR under next ch, 1 SS in 3rd of 8 ch at beginning this round.

If required, continue in this way, working 4 extra tr on each side on every round.

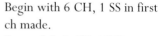

JOINING SHAPES

Triangle in Trebles
Triangles may be joined edge to edge with one of the seams on pages 24–25.

Diamond Scales
Join diamond scales edge to edge with one of the seams on pages 24–25.

Diamond scale

Colours may be changed at the beginning of any row.

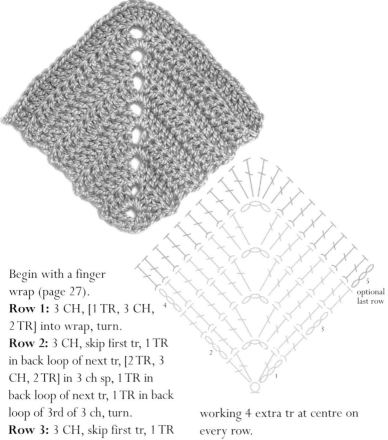

Begin with a finger wrap (page 27).

Row 1: 3 CH, [1 TR, 3 CH, 2 TR] into wrap, turn.

Row 2: 3 CH, skip first tr, 1 TR in back loop of next tr, [2 TR, 3 CH, 2 TR] in 3 ch sp, 1 TR in back loop of next tr, 1 TR in back loop of 3rd of 3 ch, turn.

Row 3: 3 CH, skip first tr, 1 TR in back loop of each tr to corner, [2 TR, 3 CH, 2 TR] in 3 ch sp, 1 TR in back loop of each tr, ending 1 TR in back loop of 3rd of 3 ch, turn.

Repeat row 3 as required, working 4 extra tr at centre on every row.

Optional last row: 3 CH, 1 TR in back loop of each tr to corner, 6 TR in 3 ch sp, 1 TR in back loop of each tr, ending 1 TR in back loop of 3rd of 3 ch. Fasten off.

○ chain

• slip stitch

⊥ treble

⊥ treble in back loop only (as page 30)

Ω finger wrap (as page 27)

▲ starting point

Shapes and Motifs

219

Beech leaf

Special stitches –
Front raised double treble (FRDTR) = yrh twice, insert hook (from the front) around stem of st below from right to left (page 31), complete a double treble; back raised double treble (BRDTR) = yrh twice, insert hook (from the back) around stem of st below from right to left (page 31), complete a double treble.

Foundation ch: 14 CH, make stalk: 1 SS in 2nd ch from hook, 1 SS in each of next 6 ch, make 9 CH more.

Row 1: 2 TR in 4th ch from hook, 1 TR in each of next 2 ch, 3 TR TOG over next 3 ch, 1 DTR in next ch (at top of stalk), 3 TR TOG over next 3 ch, 1 TR in each of next 2 ch, 3 TR in last ch, turn.

Row 2: 3 CH, 2 TR in first tr, 1 TR in each of next 2 tr, 3 TR TOG over next 3 sts, 1 BRDTR around stem of dtr, 3 TR TOG over next 3 sts, 1 TR in each of next 2 tr, 3 TR in 3rd of 3 ch, turn.

Row 3: 3 CH, skip first tr, 1 TR in each of next 2 tr, 3 TR TOG over next 3 sts, 1 FRDTR around stem of brdtr, 3 TR TOG over next 3 sts, 1 TR in each of next 2 tr, 1 TR in 3rd of 3 ch, turn.

Row 4: 3 CH, skip first tr, 3 TR TOG over next 3 sts, 1 BRDTR around stem of frdtr, 3 TR TOG over next 3 sts, 1 TR in 3rd of 3 ch, turn.

Row 5: 3 CH, work next 4 sts tog: [1 TR in next st, 1 FRDTR around stem of brdtr, 1 TR in next st and 1 TR in 3rd of 3 ch]. Fasten off.

Aster

Worked in 2 colours, A and B.

work in back loops of round 1

Using A, begin with 4 CH, 1 SS in first ch made.

Round 1: 1 CH, 11 DC into ring, change to B, 1 SS in first ch of round. Do not cut A.

Round 2: Join B to same place, [1 DC, 4 CH, 1 DC] in front loop of first ch of previous round, [1 DC, 4 CH, 1 DC] in front loop of each dc, ending 1 SS in first dc of round. Fasten off B. (12 small petals made.)

Round 3: Using A, work in empty back loops of round 1: [1 SS, 7 CH, 1 DC] in back loop of first ch, [1 DC, 7 CH, 1 DC] in back loop of each dc, ending 1 SS in first ss of round. Fasten off. (12 large petals made.)
The length of the small and large ch loops may be varied if desired.

Sunflower

Worked in 3 colours, A, B and C.

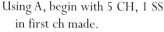

Using A, begin with 5 CH, 1 SS in first ch made.

Round 1: 3 CH, 15 TR into ring, change to B, 1 SS in 3rd of 3 ch at beginning of round. Cut A.

Round 2: Using B, 1 CH, 2 DC in space between 3 ch and first tr, [2 DC in space before next tr] 14 times, 2 DC in space before 3 ch, change to C, 1 SS in first ch of round. Cut B.

Round 3: Using C, 5 CH, skip first dc, 4 TRTR TOG, inserting hook in back loop only of each of next 4 dc, *9 CH, 5 TRTR TOG, inserting hook in same place as last insertion, then in back loop only of each of next 4 dc, repeat from * 6 more times, 9 CH, 1 SS in top of 4 trtr tog at beginning of round.

Round 4: 1 CH, 9 DC in next 9 ch sp, *skip 5 trtr tog, 9 DC in next 9 ch sp, repeat from *, ending 1 SS in first ch of round, fasten off.

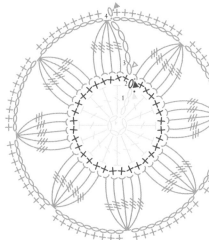

Spiral shell

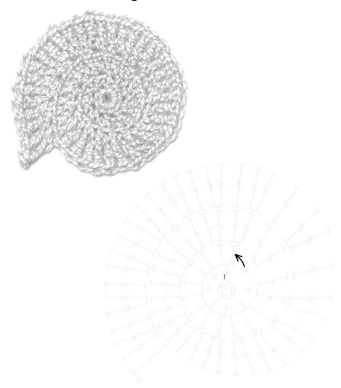

chain

•
slip stitch

+
double crochet

treble

5 triple trebles
together in
back loops only

half treble in
back loop only
(page 30)

treble in back
loop only
(page 30)

double treble in
back loop only
▲
starting point
◄
fasten off
◁
join in new
yarn

Begin with 4 CH, 1 SS in first ch made.
Round 1: 8 DC into ring. Continue in a spiral: [2 HTR in back loop of next dc] 5 times, [2 TR in back loop of next dc] 3 times, [2 TR in back loop of next htr] 6 times, [2 DTR in back loop of next htr] 4 times, [2 DTR in back loop of next tr] 3 times, [1 DTR in back loop of next tr, 2 DTR in back loop of next tr] 7 times, 1 DTR in back loop of next tr, 2 DTR in back loop of next dtr, 1 DTR in back loop of next dtr, fasten off.

SHAPES AND MOTIFS

Celtic octagon

Worked in 3 colours, A, B and C.

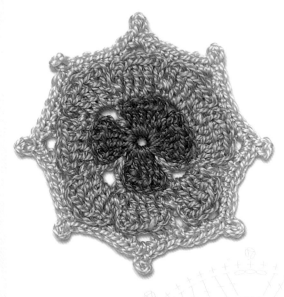

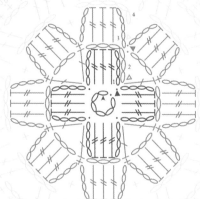

**JOINING
SHAPES**

**Celtic
Octagon**
Join on
subsequent
octagons as
you work the
last round, by
linking picots
as page 28.

The Stitch Collection

Using A, begin with 6 CH, 1 SS in first ch made.

Round 1: [4 CH, 3 DTR into ring, 4 CH, 1 SS into ring] 4 times. Fasten off A.

Round 2: Join B to same place, 6 CH, skip [4 ch, 3 dtr, 4 ch], *[1 TR, 3 CH, 1 TR] into 1 ss, 3 CH, skip [4 ch, 3 dtr, 4 ch], repeat from * twice more, 1 TR into last ss, 3 CH, 1 SS in 3rd of 6 ch at beginning of round.

Round 3: 1 CH, *4 CH, 3 DTR in 3 ch sp, 4 CH, 1 DC in next tr, repeat from * 7 more times, omitting last DC and working 1 SS in first ch of round, fasten off B.

Round 4: Join C to same place, 1 CH, *4 CH, skip [4 ch, 3 dtr, 4 ch], 1 DC in next dc, repeat from * 7 more times, omitting last DC and working 1 SS in first ch of round.

Round 5: 3 CH, *[2 TR, 3 CH, 2 TR] in 4 ch sp, 1 TR in next dc, repeat from * 7 more times, omitting last TR and working 1 SS in 3rd of 3 ch at beginning of round.

Round 6: 1 CH, 1 DC in each of next 2 tr, *2 DC in 3 ch sp, 3 CH, 1 SS in last dc made, 1 DC in same 3 ch sp, 1 DC in each of next 5 tr, repeat from * 7 more times, omitting last 5 DC and working 1 DC in each of last 2 tr, 1 SS in first ch of round, fasten off.

Arrange petals of round 3 in front of round 4, and petals of round 1 in front of round 2.

STITCH KEY

⊖
chain

·
slip stitch

+
double crochet

┬
treble

╤
double treble

▲
starting point

◄
fasten off

◁
join in new yarn

🔞
3-chain picot

Dogwood

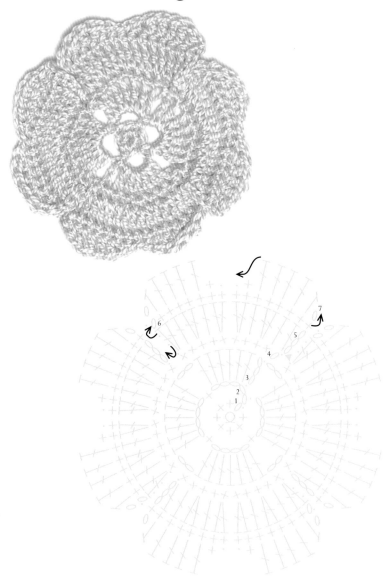

Begin with a finger wrap, (page 27).

Round 1: 1 CH, 7 DC into wrap, 1 SS in first ch of round.

Round 2: 5 CH, [skip 1 dc, 1 DC in next dc, 4 CH] 3 times, 1 SS in first ch of round.

Round 3: 1 SS in next ch, 3 CH, 6 TR under next 3 ch, 2 CH, skip 1 dc, [7 TR in next 4 ch sp, 2 CH, skip 1 dc] 3 times, 1 SS in 3rd of 3 ch at beginning of round.

Round 4: 1 CH, 1 DC in same place as last ss, [1 DC in each of next 2 tr, 2 DC in next tr] twice, skip 2 ch, *2 DC in next tr, [1 DC in each of next 2 tr, 2 DC in next tr] twice, skip 2 ch, repeat from * twice more, 1 SS in first ch of round.

Complete the first petal in rows:

Row 5: 3 CH, 1 TR in same place as last ss, [1 TR in next dc, 2 TR in next dc] twice, 2 TR in next dc, [1 TR in next dc, 2 TR in next dc] twice, turn. (= 16 tr)

Row 6: 1 CH, skip first tr, 1 DC in each of 14 tr, 1 DC in 3rd of 3 ch, turn.

Row 7: 1 CH, skip first dc, 1 HTR in next dc, 1 TR in each of next 4 dc, 1 DC in next dc, 1 SS in each of next 2 dc, 1 DC in next dc, 1 TR in each of next 4 dc, 1 HTR in last dc, 1 CH, 1 SS in 1 ch, 2 SS in side edge of tr below, 1 SS in side edge of dc below tr, 1 SS in next dc of round 4.

Repeat rows 5–7, 3 times, to complete each remaining petal in turn. Fasten off.

STITCH KEY

O
chain

.
slip stitch

+
double crochet

half treble

treble

Q
finger wrap

◀
fasten off

←
direction of working

Snowflake

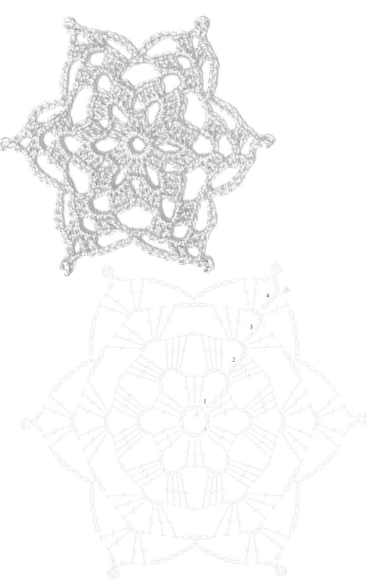

**JOINING
SHAPES**

Snowflake
 Join on
subsequent
snowflakes as
you work the
last round, by
linking picots
as page 28.

228

Begin with 9 CH, 1 SS in first ch made.

Round 1: 8 CH, 3 TR into ring, [5 CH, 3 TR into ring] 4 times, 5 CH, 2 TR into ring, 1 SS in 3rd of 8 ch at beginning of round.

Round 2: 1 SS in each of next 2 ch, 7 CH, 4 TR under next 3 ch, *1 CH, skip 3 tr, [4 TR, 4 CH, 4 TR] in 5 ch sp, repeat from * 4 more times, 1 CH, skip 3 tr, 3 TR in next ch sp, 1 SS in 3rd of 7 ch at beginning of round.

Round 3: 1 SS in each of next 2 ch, 6 CH, 3 TR under next 2 ch, 3 CH, skip [4 tr, 1 ch, 4 tr], *[3 TR, 3 CH, 3 TR] in 4 ch sp, 3 CH, skip [4 tr, 1 ch, 4 tr], repeat from * 4 more times, 2 TR in next ch sp, 1 SS in 3rd of 6 ch at beginning of round.

Round 4: 1 SS in each of next 2 ch, 8 CH, 1 SS in 4th ch from hook, 1 CH, 2 TR under next ch of previous round, 5 CH, skip 3 tr, 1 DC in 3 ch sp, *5 CH, skip 3 tr, 2 TR in 3 ch sp, 5 CH, 1 SS in 4th ch from hook, 1 CH, 2 TR in same 3 ch sp, 5 CH, skip 3 tr, 1 DC in next 3 ch sp, repeat from * 4 more times, 5 CH, skip 3 tr, 1 TR in next ch sp, 1 SS in 3rd of 8 ch at beginning of round. Fasten off.

TIP

The first 3 ch of each round stand for 1 tr.

14 Special Stitches

This section covers a variety of special effects. Broomstick stitches are formed by holding long loops on a rod, such as a large knitting needle, then working into the loops (see pages 36–37). Beads may be crocheted into the work in various designs. Open mesh grounds may be woven with contrasting colours, or overlaid with chain stitches.

Bouclé loops

Any number of sts.

TIP

It can be difficult to manipulate the hook, rod, and yarn with only two hands! Try holding the rod beneath your left arm (if you are right handed), or clamp it to a table top.

Special stitch—Bouclé loop stitch (BLS) = as page 37.
Note: A rod such as a large knitting needle is required.
Row 1: 1 DC in 2nd ch from hook, 1 DC in each ch to end, turn.
Row 2: 1 CH, lengthen this ch to height required, skip first dc, 1 BLS in each dc ending 1 BLS in 1 ch, turn.
Row 3: 1 CH, skip first bls, 1 DC in each bls ending 1 DC in 1 ch, turn.
Repeat rows 2 and 3.

Broomstick loops

Any number of sts.

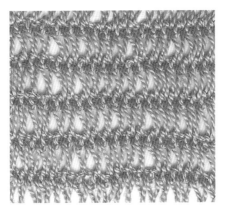

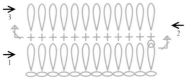

Special stitches – Loop stitch (LS) = as page 36; locking stitch (LKS) = as page 38.

Note: A rod such as a large knitting needle is required.

Row 1: Lengthen loop on hook and slip onto rod, work from left to right along the chain: skip 1 ch, *1 LS in next ch, slipping loop onto rod, repeat from * to last ch, 1 LS in last ch, lengthening loop to same height and keeping it on hook, do not turn.

Row 2: 1 LKS in ls on hook, *1 DC in next loop, slipping loop from rod, repeat from * to end, do not turn.

Row 3: Lengthen loop on hook and slip onto rod, work from left to right: skip first dc, *1 LS in next dc, slipping loop onto rod, repeat from * to last st, 1 LS in lks, lengthening loop to same height and keeping it on hook, do not turn.

Repeat rows 2 and 3.

STITCH KEY

o
chain

+
double crochet

do not turn

→
direction of work

Special Stitches

loop stitch (page 36)

locking stitch (page 38)

bouclé loop stitch (page 37)

14

Broomstick lace

A multiple of 4 sts.

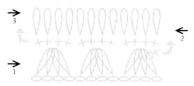

Special stitches — Loop stitch (LS) = as page 36; locking stitch (LKS) = as page 38.

Note: A rod such as a large knitting needle is required.

Row 1: Lengthen loop on hook and slip onto rod, work from left to right along the chain: skip 1 ch, *1 LS in next ch, slipping loop onto rod, repeat from * to last ch, 1 LS in last ch, lengthening loop to same height and keeping it on hook, do not turn.

Row 2: 1 LKS in ls on hook, insert hook through loop below hook and next 3 loops together (slipping loops from rod) and work 1 DC, work 3 more DC in same place, *inserting hook through next 4 loops together (slipping loops from rod) work 4 DC in same place, repeat from * to end, do not turn.

Row 3: Lengthen loop on hook and slip onto rod, work from left to right: skip first dc, *1 LS in next dc, slipping loop onto rod, repeat from *, ending in last dc, lengthen loop to same height and keep it on hook, do not work into lks, do not turn.

Repeat rows 2 and 3.

Broomstick clusters

A multiple of 5 sts + 2 (add 1 for foundation ch).

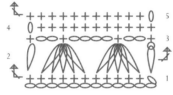

Special stitches – Loop stitch (LS) = as page 36; locking stitch (LKS) = as page 38.

Note: A rod such as a large knitting needle is required.

Row 1: 1 DC in 3rd ch from hook, 1 DC in each ch to end, do not turn.

Row 2: Lengthen loop on hook and slip onto rod, work from left to right: skip first dc, *1 LS in next dc, slipping loop onto rod, repeat from *, ending 1 LS in 1 ch, lengthening loop to same height and keeping it on hook, do not turn.

Row 3: 1 LKS in ls on hook, 2 CH, *insert hook through next 5 loops together (slipping loops from rod) and work 1 DC, 4 CH, repeat from *, ending 2 CH, 1 DC in last ls, turn.

Row 4: 1 CH, skip first dc, 2 DC in 2 ch sp, *1 DC in next dc, 4 DC in 4 ch sp, repeat from *, ending 2 DC in 2 ch sp, 1 DC in lks, turn.

Row 5: 1 CH, skip first dc, 1 DC in each dc ending 1 DC in 1 ch, do not turn.
Repeat rows 2–5.

Offset broomstick lace

A multiple of 6 sts (add 1 for foundation ch).

Special stitches – Extended loop stitch (ELS) = insert hook as directed, yrh, pull loop through, yrh, pull through, lengthen loop and slip it onto rod; locking stitch (LKS) = as page 38.

Note: A rod such as a large knitting needle is required.

Row 1: 1 DC in 2nd ch from hook, 1 DC in each ch to end, do not turn.

Row 2: 1 CH, lengthen loop on hook and slip onto rod, work from left to right: skip first dc, *1 ELS in next dc, slipping loop onto rod, repeat from *, ending 1 ELS in last dc, lengthening loop to same height and keeping it on hook, do not turn.

Row 3: 1 LKS in loop on hook, insert hook through loop below hook and next 5 loops together (slipping loops from rod) and work 5 DC in same place, *insert hook through next 6 loops together (slipping loops from rod) and work 6 DC in same place, repeat from * to end, do not turn.

Row 4: As row 2, working last ELS in lks.

Row 5: 1 LKS in loop on hook, insert hook through loop below hook and next 2 loops together (slipping loops from rod) and work 2 DC in same place, *insert hook through next 6 loops together (slipping loops from rod) and work 6 DC in same place, repeat from *, ending 3 DC in last 3 loops together, do not turn.

Repeat rows 2–5.

STITCH KEY

◯
chain

+
double crochet

do not turn

Special Stitches

locking stitch
(page 38)

extended loop
stitch

6 extended loop stitches (grouped together on following row)

Beads on double crochet

A multiple of 4 sts + 1.

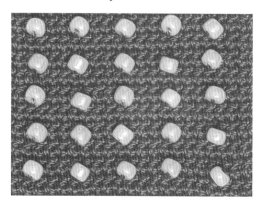

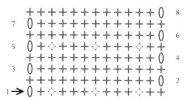

Special stitch – Bead on double crochet (BDC) = insert hook as directed, yrh, pull loop through, slide bead up yarn close to work, yrh (catching yarn beyond bead), pull through both loops on hook.

Begin by threading all beads required onto yarn.

Work at least 3 rows of double crochet as page 17.

Row 1 (wrong side row): 1 CH, skip first dc, 1 DC in next dc, *1 BDC in next dc, 1 DC in each of next 3 dc, repeat from *, ending 1 DC in last dc, 1 DC in 1 ch, turn.

Row 2: 1 CH, skip first dc, 1 DC in each st ending 1 DC in 1 ch, turn.

Rows 3 and 4: As row 2. Repeat rows 1–4.

Beads on half trebles

Odd number of sts.

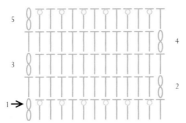

Special stitch – Bead on half treble (BHTR) = yrh, insert hook as directed, yrh, pull loop through, slide bead up yarn close to work, yrh (catching yarn beyond bead), pull through 3 loops on hook.

Begin by threading all beads required onto yarn.

Work at least 3 rows of half trebles as page 19.

Row 1 (wrong side row): 2 CH, skip first htr, *1 BHTR in next htr, 1 HTR in next htr, repeat from *, working last HTR in 2nd of 2 ch, turn.

Row 2: 2 CH, skip first htr, 1 HTR in each st ending 1 HTR in 2nd of 2 ch, turn.

Rows 3 and 4: As row 2.

Repeat rows 1–4.

Beads on trebles

A multiple of 6 sts + 1.

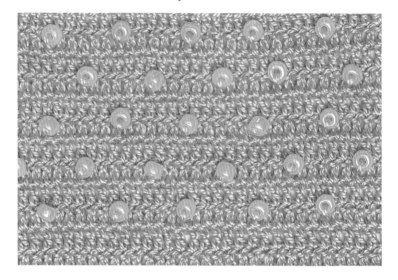

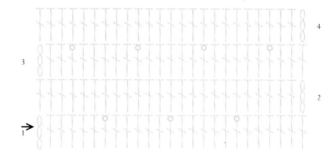

Special stitch – Bead on treble (BTR) = yrh, insert hook as directed, yrh, pull loop through, yrh, pull through 2 loops, slide bead up yarn close to work, yrh (catching yarn beyond bead), pull through both loops on hook.

Begin by threading all beads required onto yarn.

Work at least 1 row of trebles as page 19.

Row 1 (wrong side row) : 3 CH, skip first tr, 1 TR in each of next 5 tr, *1 BTR in next tr, 1 TR in each of next 5 tr, repeat from *, ending 1 TR in each of last 5 tr, 1 TR in 3rd of 3 ch, turn.

Row 2: 3 CH, skip first tr, 1 TR in each st ending 1 TR in 3rd of 3 ch, turn.

Row 3: 3 CH, skip first tr, 1 TR in each of next 2 tr, *1 BTR in next tr, 1 TR in each of next 5 tr, repeat from * to last 4 sts, 1 BTR in next tr, 1 TR in each of last 2 tr, 1 TR in 3rd of 3 ch, turn.

Row 4: As row 2.

Repeat rows 1–4.

TIPS

Beads may be arranged on double crochet, half trebles, or trebles in any design to form a regular repeating pattern or a single motif; they should always be placed on a wrong side row.

Beads may also be added to any other stitch pattern. On a wrong side row, push a bead close up to the work before the last "yrh, pull through" that completes the required stitch.

STITCH KEY

O
chain

T
treble

→
direction of working

Special Stitch

bead on treble

Woven checks

A multiple of 6 sts + 1 (add 2 for foundation ch).

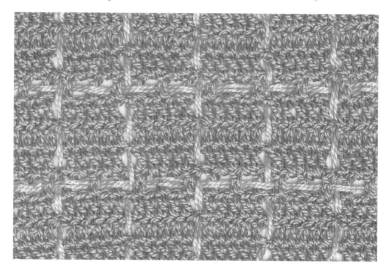

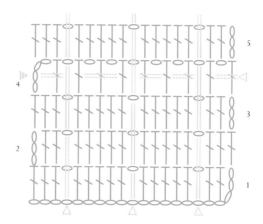

Note: A tapestry needle is required for the weaving. Worked in 2 colours, A and B. Use A to work the crochet ground:

Row 1: 1 TR in 4th ch from hook, 1 TR in next ch, *1 CH, skip 1 ch, 1 TR in each of next 5 ch, repeat from *, ending 1 TR in each of last 3 ch, turn.

Row 2: 3 CH, skip first tr, 1 TR in each of next 2 tr, 1 CH, skip 1 ch, *1 TR in each of next 5 tr, 1 CH, skip 1 ch, repeat from *, ending 1 TR in each of last 2 tr, 1 TR in 3rd of 3 ch, turn.

Row 3: As row 2.

Row 4: 4 CH, skip first 2 tr, 1 TR in next tr, 1 CH, skip 1 ch, * [1 TR in next tr, 1 CH, skip 1 tr] twice, 1 TR in next tr, 1 CH, skip 1 ch, repeat from *, ending 1 TR in next tr, 1 CH, skip 1 tr, 1 TR in 3rd of 3 ch, turn.

Row 5: 3 CH, skip first tr, 1 TR in ch sp, 1 TR in next tr, 1 CH, skip 1 ch, * [1 TR in next tr, 1 tr in ch sp] twice, 1 TR in next tr, 1 CH, skip 1 ch, repeat from *,

ending 1 TR in next tr, 1 TR under 4 ch, 1 TR in 3rd of these 4 ch, turn.

Repeat rows 2–5 as required. Use B to work the weaving: Double a length of yarn and thread the two ends into tapestry needle. Pass needle through first ch sp of row 1, then through loop of yarn to secure. Bring needle up through ch sp of row 1, down through ch sp of row 2, then up and down through the ch sps up to top edge. Stretch the work gently to ensure weaving is not too tight, then fasten off. Work the next line in a similar way, but begin by taking needle down through ch sp of row 1 and up through ch sp of row 2. Repeat these 2 lines all across the work.

Then work all the horizontal lines of weaving in a similar way, through the ch sps of each repeat of row 4.

Woven mesh

Odd number of sts (add 3 for foundation ch).

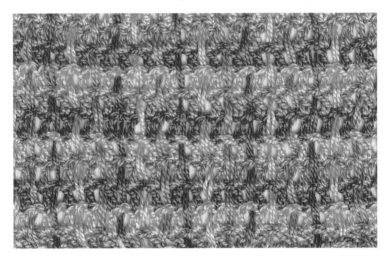

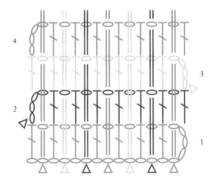

Notes: A tapestry needle is required for the weaving. Change colours at end of each row in same way as for 3-colour, one-row stripes, (see page 183). Worked in 3 colours, A, B and C. Begin with foundation ch in A.

Row 1: 1 TR in 6th ch from hook, *1 CH, skip 1 ch, 1 TR in next ch, repeat from *, changing to B at end of row, turn.

Row 2: 4 CH, skip [first tr and 1 ch], *1 TR in next tr, 1 CH, skip 1 ch, repeat from *, ending 1 TR in 4th of 5 ch and changing to C, turn.

Row 3: As row 2, working last TR in 3rd of 4 ch and changing to A.

Repeat row 3, changing to next colour at end of each row.

To work the weaving, double a length of A and thread the two ends into tapestry needle. Pass needle through first ch sp of row 1, then through loop of yarn to secure. Take needle down through ch sp of row 1, up through ch sp of row 2, then up and down through the ch sps up to top edge. Stretch the work gently to ensure weaving is not too tight, then fasten off. Work the next line in B a similar way, but begin by bringing needle up through ch sp of row 1 and down through ch sp of row 2. Repeat these 2 lines all across the work, using C for next line, then A, B and C in order throughout.

TIP

The ends of the weaving yarns may be used to make a knotted fringe along the edge of the work. You can of course work the weaving from top to bottom, to make a fringed lower edge, or begin the weaving by leaving long ends so that a fringe may be knotted at both top and bottom.

STITCH KEY

○
chain

treble

weaving yarn

△
join in new
colour

Overlaid checks

A multiple of 8 sts + 1 (add 2 for foundation ch).

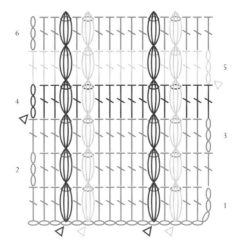

Special stitch – Overlaid chain (OCH) = with yarn at back of work and right side of work facing, insert hook in next ch sp, catch yarn at back of work and pull through loop on hook (see page 39).

Worked in 3 colours, A, B and C.

Begin with foundation ch in A.

Row 1: 1 TR in 4th ch from hook, 1 TR in next ch, *1 CH, skip 1 ch, 1 TR in next ch, 1 CH, skip 1 ch, 1 TR in each of next 5 ch, repeat from *, ending 1 TR in each of last 3 ch, turn.

Row 2: 3 CH, skip first tr, 1 TR in each of next 2 tr, *1 CH, skip 1 ch, 1 TR in next tr, 1 CH, skip 1 ch, 1 TR in each of next 5 tr, repeat from *, ending 1 TR in each of last 2 tr, 1 TR in 3rd of 3 ch, turn.

Row 3: As row 2, changing to B (as page 23) at end of row.

Row 4: As row 2, changing to C at end of row.

Row 5: As row 2, changing to A at end of row.

Row 6: As row 2.

Repeat rows 2–6 as required.

To work the overlay, begin at bottom of right hand line of ch sps: using B double, join to empty foundation ch, 1 OCH in first ch sp of line, * lengthen loop on hook to height of 1 row, 1 OCH in next ch sp above, repeat from * to top of work, fasten off. Using C double, join to empty foundation ch at bottom of next line of ch sps and work overlay in same way up to top edge.

Repeat these 2 lines across the work, filling all the lines of ch sps.

TIP

This technique is also known as Surface Crochet. On a plain mesh background designs of many kinds may be built up using overlaid chains in one or more colours.

STITCH KEY

o
chain

⊥
treble

Δ
join in new colour

Special Stitch

overlaid chain (page 39)

Overlaid steps

Odd number of sts (add 3 for foundation ch).

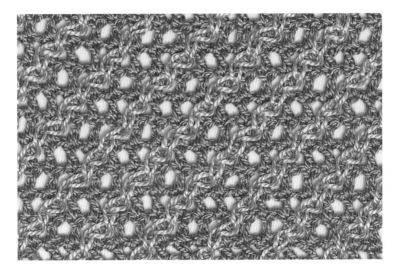

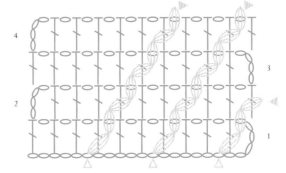

Special stitch – Overlaid chain (OCH) = with yarn at back of work and right side of work facing, insert hook in next ch sp as directed, catch yarn at back of work and pull through loop on hook (see page 39).

Worked in 2 colours, A and B. Use A to work the background mesh:

Row 1: 1 TR in 6th ch from hook, *1 CH, skip 1 ch, 1 TR in next ch, repeat from * to end, turn.

Row 2: 4 CH, skip [first tr and 1 ch], 1 TR in next tr, *1 CH, skip 1 ch, 1 TR in next tr, repeat from *, working last TR in 4th of 5 ch, turn.

Row 3: As row 2, working last TR in 3rd of 4 ch.

Repeat row 3 as required.

To work the overlay, begin at bottom edge (it is a good idea to begin at the centre): using B double, join to empty foundation ch of any ch sp, lengthen loop on hook to width of 1 mesh, 1 OCH in next ch sp to right, * lengthen loop on hook to height of 1 row, 1 OCH in next ch sp above, lengthen loop on hook to width of 1 mesh, 1 OCH in next ch sp to right, repeat from * to top of work, fasten off. Work more stepped lines of overlaid chain to right and left, spacing as desired.

TIP

Designs are easily plotted on graph paper, using the squares of the paper to represent the mesh background.

STITCH KEY

o
chain

丅
treble

Δ
join in new colour

▶
fasten off

Special Stitch

overlaid chain
(page 39)

Abbreviations and Symbols

These are the abbreviations and symbols used in this book. There is no worldwide standard, so, in other publications, you may find different abbreviations and symbols.

Throughout this book, abbreviations in CAPITAL LETTERS are the stitches you make on the current row or round, and abbreviations in lower-case letters are used for the stitches of previous rows or rounds to describe where the hook is inserted.

Basic stitches, abbreviations, and symbols

English crochet terms are used throughout this book, abbreviated as shown. For detailed methods of working, see pages 16-41.

Stitch	Abbreviation	Symbol
stitch(es)	st(s)	(none)
chain	CH, ch	o
slip stitch	SS, ss	·
double crochet	DC, dc	+
extended double crochet	EXDC, exdc	⊥
half treble	HTR, htr	T
treble	TR, tr	⟊
double treble	DTR, dtr	⟊
triple treble	TRTR, trtr	⟊
chain space	ch sp	(none)
together	TOG, tog	(none)
yarn round hook	yrh	(none)

Special abbreviations

In addition, various stitch patterns use special stitch constructions and, where these occur in this book, the abbreviation and symbol used are indicated in the Special Stitch instructions for that pattern. Sometimes abbreviations may be combined, e.g., SCL or scl means spike cluster; RP or rp means raised popcorn. Always refer to Special Stitch instructions where they occur. Any published pattern should include a list of all the abbreviations and symbols used, which may differ from those given below.

Stitch	Abbreviation	Symbol	Stitch	Abbreviation	Symbol
loop stitch	LS, ls		Tunisian knit stitch	TKS, tks	
locking stitch	LKS, lks		Tunisian purl stitch	TPS, tps	
extended loop stitch	ELS, els		group	GP, gp	(none)
bouclé loop stitch	BLS, bls		cluster	CL, cl	
overlaid chain	OCH		pineapple or puff stitch	PS, ps	
front raised double crochet	FRDC, frdc		popcorn	PC, pc or P, p	
front raised treble	FRTR, frtr		bullion stitch	BS, bs	
back raised treble	BRTR, brtr		reverse double crochet	REV DC, rev dc	
front raised double treble	FRDTR, frdtr		spike	S; s	e.g.
			Solomon's knot	SK, sk	
Tunisian simple stitch	TSS, tss		Finger wrap	(none)	

Additional symbols

These are used on some charts to clarify the meaning.

Description	Symbol
starting point	▲
join in new yarn	▽
fasten off yarn	▼
direction of working	→
do not turn work	↱→
stitch worked in front loop only	⊥ ⌶
stitch worked in back loop only	⊤ ⌶

Arrangement of symbols

Description	Symbol	Explanation
symbols joined at top	×× ⋀ ⋀	A group of symbols may be joined at the top, indicating that these stitches should be worked together as a cluster, as page 32.
symbols joined at base	⋁ ⋁ ⋎	Symbols joined at the base should all be worked into the same stitch below, as page 29.
symbols joined at top and bottom	⬙ ⬙ ⬭	Sometimes a group of stitches is joined at both top and bottom, making a puff, bobble, or popcorn, as pages 33–34.
symbols on a curve	⁺⁺⁺⁺	Sometimes symbols are drawn along a curve, depending on the construction of the stitch pattern.
distorted symbols	ϯ Ϝ ⌡	Some symbols may be lengthened, curved or spiked to indicate where the hook is inserted below, as for Spike stitches, page 30.

English/American equivalent terms

Some American terms differ from the English system, as shown below: patterns published using American terminology can be very confusing unless you understand the difference.

English	American	American Abbreviation	Symbol
double crochet	single crochet	SC, sc	+
extended double	extended single	EXSC, exsc	
half treble	half double	HDC, hdc	
treble	double	DC, dc	
double treble	treble	TR, tr	
triple treble	double treble	DTR, dtr	

TIP

Remember that a chart represents how a stitch pattern is constructed, and may not bear much resemblance to the actual appearance of the finished stitch. Always read the written instructions together with the chart.

Glossary

Back (of work) The side of the work away from you as you work the current row or round.

Bobble (stitch) Several stitches worked in the same place and joined together at the top, often on a background of shorter stitches (page 33): compare Puff (stitch).

Broomstick crochet A particular type of crochet, worked with both a crochet hook and a "broomstick" such as a large knitting needle (page 36).

Cluster (stitch) Several stitches worked together at the top.

Cotton (yarn) Spun from the fibres of cotton plants.

Crochet A continuous thread worked into a fabric of interlocking loops with the aid of a hook; the act of working such a fabric.

Edging Decorative crochet rows worked along the edge(s) of a main piece (pages 125–129).

Fan (stitch) Several stitches worked into the same place, so joined at the base to make a fan, or shell, shape (pages 73–85).

Foundation chain The initial length of chain stitches used to begin most crochet work.

Front (of work) The side of the work facing you as you work the current row or round.

Gauge The number of stitches and rows to a given measurement (page 42).

Hook, crochet hook The tool used for most crochet work: a slim shaft of metal, wood, or plastic with a hook at one end, available in many sizes (pages 10–11).

Knitting needle Normally used in pairs for knitting: a slim shaft of metal, wood, or plastic with a smooth point at one end and a knob at the other, available in many sizes (page 14).

Lace (stitch pattern) A stitch pattern forming an openwork design (pages 98–124).

Linen (yarn) Spun from the fibres of flax plants.

Lurex (yarn) A metallic-effect yarn, normally spun from polyester and viscose.

Mercerised (yarn) Chemically treated to improve strength, lustre, and reception to dye.

Mesh (stitch pattern) A stitch pattern forming a regular geometric grid.

Natural fibre (yarn) Any yarn derived from animal products (such as wool) or vegetable products (such as cotton or linen).

Overlaid (stitches) Crochet chains (or other stitches) worked on top of a crochet mesh background (page 39).

Puff (stitch) Several stitches (often half trebles/trebles) worked in the same place, and joined together at the top (page 33): compare Bobble (stitch).

Raised (stitches) Stitches formed by inserting the hook around the stem of a stitch below the normal position (page 31).

Relief (stitches) Another name for Raised stitches.

Right side (of work) The side of the work that will be the right side of the finished piece.

Shell (stitch) See Fan (stitch).

Silk (yarn) Spun from the unravelled cocoons of the silkworm.

Spike (stitch) A stitch worked by inserting the hook from front to back, one or more rows below the normal position, and/or to the right or left (page 30).

Synthetic (yarn) Spun from fibres derived from coal and petroleum products, to resemble natural fibre yarns.

Tapestry needle A needle with a large eye and blunt tip (page 14).

Tricot needle Another name for a Tunisian hook.

Trim A length of crochet worked separately and sewn to a main piece, or onto plain fabric, as a decoration (pages 130–136).

Tunisian crochet A particular type of crochet, worked back and forth in rows without turning the work (page 40).

Tunisian hook The tool used for Tunisian crochet: a long, slim shaft of metal, wood, or plastic with a hook at one end and a knob at the other (page 11).

Viscose (yarn) Spun from a man-made fibre manufactured from cellulose.

Wool (yarn) Spun from the fleece of sheep.

Wrong side (of work) The side of the work that will be the wrong side of the finished piece.

Index

I n d e x

Credits

The author would like to thank DMC Creative World for kindly supplying the yarns used in the Stitch Collection. Also thanks to Coats Crafts UK for the hooks and accessories.